HAVE A TURTLE-IFIC DAY!

INSPIRATIONAL MESSAGES FOR TURTLE LOVERS

KATHLEEN J. SHIELDS

Have A Turtle-ific Day – Inspirational Messages for Turtle Lovers
© Copyright 2025 Kathleen J. Shields

No portion of this book may be reproduced, stored in a retrieval system, or transmitted in any form or by any means—electronic, mechanical, photocopy, recording, scanning, or other—except for brief quotations and critical reviews or articles, without the prior written permission of the author or publisher. Cover turtle photo c/o Darsi-uwphoto Pixabay.

ISBN: 978-1-956581-53-9

Canyon Lake, Texas
www.ErinGoBraghPublishing.com

FOR DENICE,

Because you KNEW I had it in me!

TABLE OF CONTENTS

A Brief Education about Turtles 1
Be Like A Turtle 6
Learn From Baby Turtles 18
Ocean Puns 33
Soak Up the Sunlight 49
Swim with the Tide 67
It's All About the Climb 80
Relax & Slow Down 96
Sleep Restores Your Soul 108
Dream Big 119
Stay Out of Trouble 133
Uniquely You 149
Ever-lasting Messages 162
About the Author 187

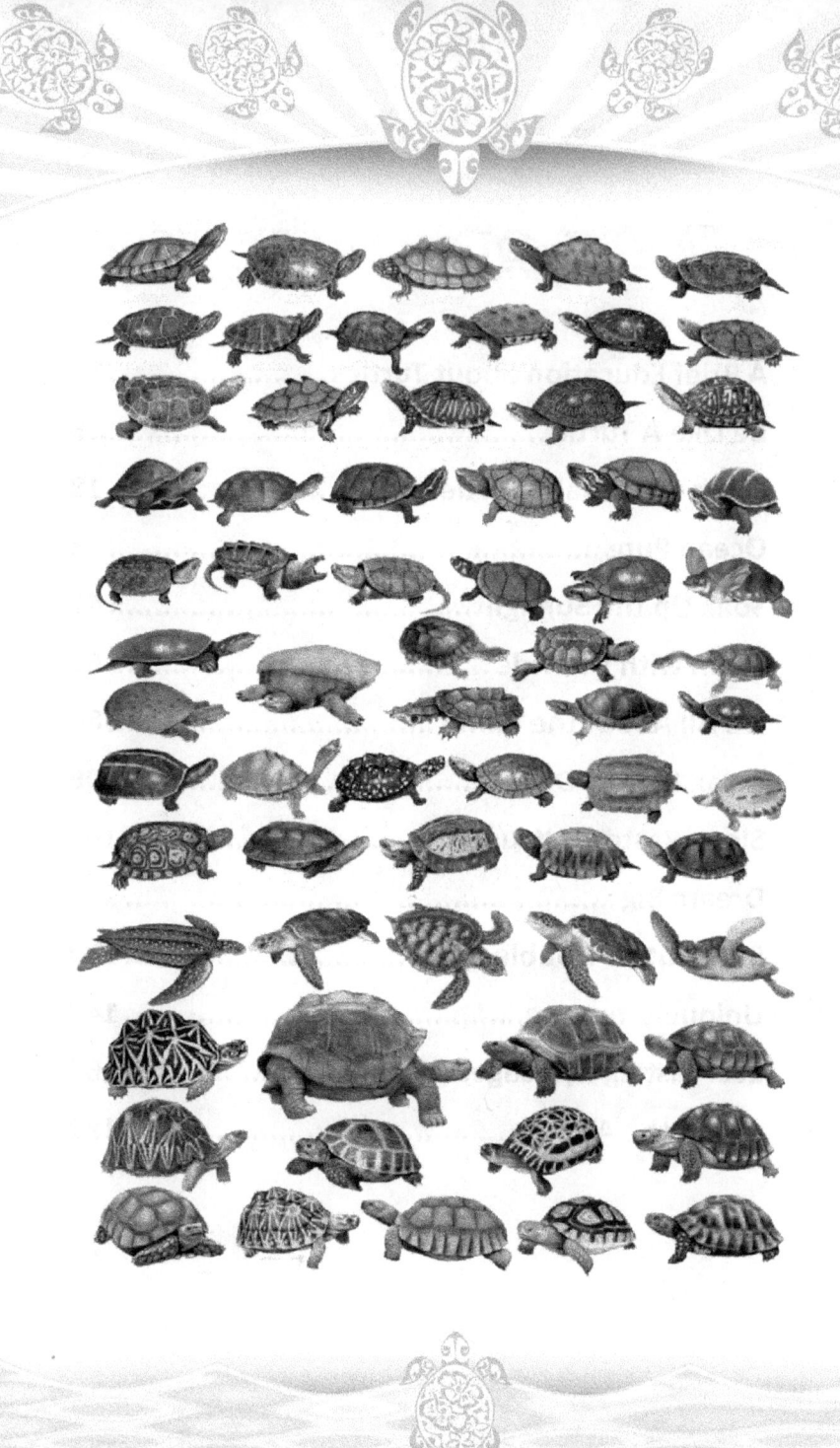

A Brief Education About Turtles

There are over 356 different species of turtles and tortoises in the world, and it is important to note that all tortoises are turtles but not all turtles are tortoises. If that doesn't seem confusing, there is such a huge variety of species, that the fascinating facts about them is almost endless.

Turtles are cold-blooded reptiles. They are widely distributed across the world's continents, oceans, deserts and islands with terrestrial, fully aquatic, and semi-aquatic species. They all lay eggs in the sand and the egg sizes depend on the size of the turtle laying them. Some small and some large.

Turtles can be swimmers but some stay on land, while tortoises almost always stay on land. A quick reference is the difference in shell height. The taller domed shells tend to be land-going tortoises while the lower, more streamlined shells are better for swimming through the water.

There are 7 Sea Turtle species that are marine aquatic, living their entire lives in the ocean. The females are the only ones that emerge every few years to lay eggs on the beach. They have flippers to be more hydrodynamic and some of their shells can be hard while some have a leathery shell.

There are 330 freshwater aquatic turtle species, the most common being the Red-Eared Slider. With webbed feet and a smooth, hydrodynamic shells, they can swim effortlessly through the shallow waters of ponds and rivers. Most have hard shells, though some have soft shells. They live in rivers, lakes, streams, swamps and ponds. They bask on the water's edge or on floating logs and inhabit a variety of freshwater habitats around the world.

There are 25 species of soft-shelled turtles which are also freshwater turtles but they are characterized by their pliable, leathery, somewhat flexible shells. The lack of a hard shell makes them more agile allowing them to swim faster.

There are 7 types of box turtles which get their name from their high domed top shell and large, hinged bottom shell which allows the turtle to close itself up to protect from predators. When they seal their shell closed, they become an impregnable box. There are four recognized species and their feet are not webbed since they live on land.

There are around 56 tortoise species which are terrestrial reptiles, meaning they are exclusively land creatures. They have heavily armored and column shaped feet with claws that look more like elephant feet. They can be found in deserts, arid grasslands and even evergreen forests.

Why are box turtles not tortoises?

While box turtles don't swim, and their shells are domed and feet are more club-like, they are not considered tortoises. Box turtles still have some webbing on their feet while tortoise feet are like stumpy elephant feet. Box turtles like moist environments while tortoises like dry, and oddly enough box turtles are way more social than tortoises that prefer a solitary lifestyle.

Can all turtles retract their necks?

No. **Turtle necks** differ in each species. Some turtles can pull or retract their neck into their shell either backwards or sideways to hide while others cannot retract their heads at all. Sea turtles have mostly lost their ability to retract their heads. Some other aquatic turtles can extend and wrap their neck around their body like an African side neck or an Alligator Snapping Turtle. Adapting to their environment, each turtle has their own shape and style.

Turtles come in all shapes and sizes.

Some of the **smallest turtle** species are the Musk Turtle, the Mississippi Mud turtle, and the Bog turtle reaching no more than 4 inches in length You think they look cute as adult turtles; you should see how teeny tiny they are as babies! Cutest little tykes ever! The **largest** freshwater turtle is the Alligator Snapping Turtle which could weigh up to 400 pounds. And then there are large land tortoises, like the Aldabra which can get up to 800 pounds, the Galapagos which live a span of 150 years and weight approximately 880 pounds and the Sulcata which can grow up to 200 pounds.

That being said, there are also large sea turtles like the Green Sea Turtle that can get to 1100 pounds, the Loggerhead can get to 1200 pounds and the Leatherback which is the largest turtle in the world reaching lengths of seven feet and weighing more than 2000 pounds!

What else should you know?

Now that you're a turtle trivia expert, let's explore their lifestyles and discover how YOU can learn important life lessons from these incredible creatures that have traversed the Earth for over 200 million years! Turtles are remarkable not only for their longevity but also for their incredible adaptability. They thrive in diverse environments, from oceans to deserts, showcasing their ability to navigate various challenges. With their hard shells providing protection and their slow, steady nature helping them endure, turtles exemplify the strength of perseverance. Their hardiness serves as a powerful reminder for us to embrace change and adapt to life's challenges with patience and courage!

Be Like a Turtle

BE LIKE A TURTLE, AT EASE IN YOUR OWN SHELL

Did you know that turtle shells are part of their body? Unlike snails and hermit crabs which can come out of their shell, turtles cannot. Contrary to what the cartoons show. Turtles carry their homes everywhere they go. They grow up always carrying their weight as they travel through the long distances of life. They are comfortable and at ease in their own shell because it is all that they have. You should be comfortable in your own skin because that is precisely what God gave you. Be like a turtle. Don't carry more than what was given to you, don't over burden yourself taking on more than you need to, and don't try to trade your shell in for anything. Your turtle shell is perfect, just like you, because it was made for you.

SEEK THE LIGHT AND BASK IN IT

Water turtles love to bask. They climb out of the water after a long swim to dry out their body under the sunlight. Warming their bodies, absorbing those excellent nutrients and absorbing the UV. A healthy turtle will bask every day for hours, and you should too! Maybe not for hours, but you should definitely go outside, soak up some of that sun, warm up and absorb some of those wonderful warm rays.

Your body wants and requires it and the rest and relaxation will do you a world of good.

Home is Where Your Shell is

The turtle shell reminds us that relaxation and peace are not bound by location but are carried within. The turtle carries its home wherever it goes. This teaches us that relaxation and contentment come from creating a sense of peace inside of ourselves.

Your shell is not just a physical space; it's a sanctuary of inner calm and solace. Retreat into your own inner shell. Find moments of stillness and comfort, no matter where you are, and let this personal sanctuary be your place of rest and rejuvenation.

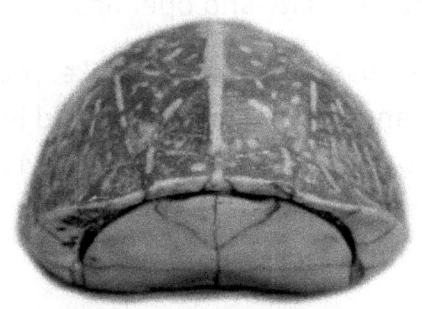

A HARD SHELL IS NOT A HARD HEAD

I hear this message coming from the mouth of a wise old turtle talking with some young whippersnapper just born whose belly button has only just disappeared.

"I want to explore the world. I want to swim to the deep end. I want to be able to climb to the top of the pyramid." Just because you want to do it, doesn't mean you are ready or that you should.

Having a hard head, saying no, refusing to listen to sage advice will only prove you're not ready.

True strength lies not in stubbornness or rigidity, but in its adaptability and openness.

So just because you may feel like you're ready, hard shell and all, maybe you should listen to the advice of others and then make a wise decision about how to proceed.

STAY CALM UNDER PRESSURE

When baby turtles are born weather land turtles, aquatic turtles or sea turtles they must emerge from eggs buried deep underground. Sometimes it is just moist sand that they must climb up, sometimes it is hard dirt that has been compacted over time.

When they come out of their eggs it is dark, and they must start digging. They must dig upwards moving dirt as they go causing pressure all around them. But once their paws, claws or fins break through the surface, the light shines down on them and they are able to move forward.

No matter how difficult that first step may be, as long as you are moving towards the light, you will be just fine.

EVEN THICK SKIN CAN GET CUT

You may think you are tough and ornery. You may put strong appearance but even the meanest turtle can get cut. Barreling through life, refusing to change their mindset, they will push through a barbed fence if they are determined enough to get to the other side.

But just because you are fixated with an insatiable resolve doesn't mean barreling into the unknown or pushing through barriers is the best route to go. Sometimes obstacles are presented to protect you. You may find a better, safer, easier way to get there if you look carefully and take it all into consideration. Don't get cut by life because you won't slow down and take it all in. You don't want to get cut when you don't have to.

Don't Retreat Into Your Shell

Some turtles can retreat into their shells, some cannot. While the turtle's shell offers a refuge, it's meant to be a place of temporary solace, not a permanent escape. Retreating is not the answer to life's challenges.

When faced with difficulties, your instinct might be to withdraw, to hide away in the safety of your comfort zone. Trust me, I have felt that way for years now! But true growth and character come from engaging with the world, not retreating from it. Embrace the challenges as opportunities.

Let your shell be the place where you gather clarity, but don't let it become a barrier that isolates you from life's experiences.

Think Long Term, Life is a Long Journey

Imagine you're a desert tortoise. It's a hot sunny day. You're taking a long journey across the desert. With each step, you display boldness, purpose and patience. Gracefully navigating the hot, dry rocky landscape one step at a time with the weight of your home on your shoulders. Sounds exhausting, right?

At least in my yard, my tortoises have ample shade to escape into, but Texas summers still get hot. The sun still finds holes to shine through and the tortoises still need to pick up and move to a shadier spot every now and then. Sure, when it gets hot, they slow down, but it is to ration the amount of energy they exert.

The desert tortoise teaches us that the beauty of our own journey is all about the slow, deliberate moments. We should meet every challenge with a calm demeanor and every milestone should be savored with appreciation.

The tortoise's enduring spirit should inspire you to embrace life's path with a steady resolve and a quiet confidence. As you traverse along your own unique journey, remember that every moment, whether sunlit or shadowed, contributes to the rich tapestry of your grand adventure.

Find strength in your persistence, joy in your journey, and serenity along each step you take. Your life is a grand voyage, even if it feels as if you are stuck in the desert, standing still, and sweltering in the hot sun.

Don't Get Weighed Down

A turtle's shell, though protective, can become cumbersome when out of the water. Life's challenges can begin to feel overwhelming if you let them pile up.

While the shell provides essential protection and a sense of security, it's crucial for the turtle (and for you) to balance weight with a sense of freedom and ease. If you carry the weight of the world on your back it will slow you down. It will make every step you take seem heavy. Instead, strive to navigate life's journey with a light heart and a flexible spirit.

Unburden yourself from whatever is weighing you down. Do this, so you can soar, glide or swim into your next adventure.

AGE GRACEFULLY, WHERE WILL YOU BE IN 100 YEARS?

Turtles come in all shapes and sizes. Some turtles stay very small their entire life, while other turtles can get very big. But the neat thing about turtles is the fact that the older they get, the smoother their shell becomes. Turtles age gracefully, losing the ripples of their carapace. My aunt had a turtle that was 100 years old. His shell was as smooth as a bowling ball, when his younger friends had very clear pyramiding and scutes.

Their enduring presence in the natural world is a testament to their perseverance and wisdom.

Each line and curve on its shell tells a story of time well spent, a life marked by patience and perseverance. Until the lines become so fine, they blend together into a harmoniously smooth masterpiece. Just like you will.

Learn From Baby Turtles

DIG YOURSELF OUT OF A HOLE YOU DIDN'T DIG

Frustrated that you have items on your to do list that you feel shouldn't be there? Sometimes you have to dig yourself out of a hole that you didn't dig. Like baby turtles all across the globe, they are born in eggs buried deep within the ground, months earlier, and their first steps are expected on day one.

Whether it is compacted sand or dried, hard dirt, every turtle must dig their way out before they can emerge from within to see the light for the first time. Is it fair? What is fair in life? That's just the way it is. Buckling down, putting forth the effort and succeeding is the only way to live. Otherwise, you are just sitting in a dark hole waiting for someone to dig you out. You may have a long, dark wait. You also may perish.

NEVER FORGET WHERE YOU CAME FROM

Female sea turtles are the most fascinating when it comes to turtle eggs and babies. The fact that a tiny baby, that pecked itself out of a buried egg, can climb to the surface of its nest, traverse across an open beach full of predators, only to leap into the water for an eternal swim that will last a century, they also memorize where they were born, so they can return to it, twenty years later, to lay their own clutch of eggs.

While our journey, to start out with may be fraught full of obstacles, and you may or may not be in a hurry to get as far away from it when the time comes, don't forget to return to where you came from every once in a while, to remind yourself of your humble beginnings. They are, in fact, what made you, you.

Big Things Often Have Small Beginnings

Big turtles often have small beginnings, a profound reminder that great things often start from modest origins. When a tiny hatchling emerges from a fragile egg, its existence proves it is bound for grand adventures and big things.

This humble start is a metaphor for how grand achievements and monumental successes often begin. Every great endeavor, every significant accomplishment, starts with a small action. Every step you take, every decision you make, and every dream you've nurtured is part of your journey.

The journey may be challenging at times, but it is the small beginnings that lay the foundation for extraordinary growth.

KEEP MOVING FORWARD

It is dawn. The tiny sea turtle emerges from the cool, dark refuge of its sandy nest. Greeted by the symphony of waves, the whispers of the wind and the cries of the seagull, it takes its first step.

With bravery we can hardly contemplate, it scuttles across the sandy beach. Propelling its way through the labyrinth of obstacles that lie between it and the embrace of the sea. The tumultuous roar of the surf is both a threat and a promise, urging it forward with both peril and possibility.

As the turtle reaches the water's edge, the cool, welcoming fingers of the tide lap at its weary form. Yet its journey has only just begun. Within the ocean, the world is a grand tapestry of swirling blues. Where currents dance like invisible ballerinas to the rhythm of the sea. In this ever-moving oceanic ballet, the baby turtle grows and learns, navigating the tremendous size of the ocean with a graceful, instinctual artistry that I'm sure we all would love to have. As it matures, the turtle becomes a seasoned traveler, mastering the art of the deep, its once-tender shell now a testament to its fortitude and adaptability.

The baby sea turtle just keeps moving forward in life and so should you. No matter what obstacles get in your way, what predators surround you, and no matter how tired you are getting, you have to just keep going, because that is all you CAN do.

NEVER DISCOURAGE OTHERS WHO MAKE PROGRESS

Imagine the sea turtle's courageous journey towards growth and achievement. Each stroke leads it to new horizons. Every inch gained and every milestone reached is a victory, no matter how gradual or small.

Comparably, the turtle charts a course through the waves and learns the rhythm of the currents, so too should we honor and encourage every step of progress made by others.

Never discourage others who make progress, even if they are slow. Be like the turtle, focused and humble, triumphing in silence.

THE JOURNEY OF A THOUSAND MILES BEGINS WITH ONE STEP

The baby turtle embarks on an epic journey across a world so huge that even we feel its greatness. Each step the turtle takes, however seemingly insignificant, is crucial to reaching its destination. Maybe it's just heading to a pond or lake, maybe a river, maybe the wide, open ocean, maybe just a dry deserted desert. Either way, its journey must begin with that first step and continue with each step taken after that.

Every great adventure, every monumental achievement, everything you do in life starts with that first, bold step. So take it!

And then keep going.

EVEN SMALL TURTLES CAN MAKE WAVES

This is my butterfly effect concept. The butterfly effect is where a seemingly insignificant event; a butterfly flapping its wings, can set in motion a series of events leading to major outcomes. Those tiny flapping wings can send out concentric ripples that gradually expand outward.

A turtle's flipper splashes upon the surface of the water. It causes a ripple that continues across the vast expanse of the ocean. Small actions or events lead to significant, far-reaching consequences. It serves as a reminder that even the smallest actions can set off a chain of reactions that impact the larger world.

Embrace the potential of your small beginnings. Know that they can set off waves of change far beyond what you might ever imagine for yourself.

A butterfly drinks the tears of a turtle.

*Turtles produce tears in order to remove excess sodium from their bodies, which is needed by butterflies in the Western Amazon.
The butterflies are attracted to the turtles' tears because they contain salt, an important mineral that is not readily available in the western Amazon.*

WHEN YOU GET KNOCKED DOWN, FLIP YOURSELF OVER

When life knocks you down, channel the spirit and strength of the turtle. When a land turtle finds itself on its back, it uses its legs, neck and tail, along with pure determination to right itself and continue its journey. It doesn't matter how it happened, whether it climbed something it shouldn't have and fell on its own, or whether a predator attacked and knocked it over. The turtle's durability lies not in avoiding the fall but in its persistence to keep going.

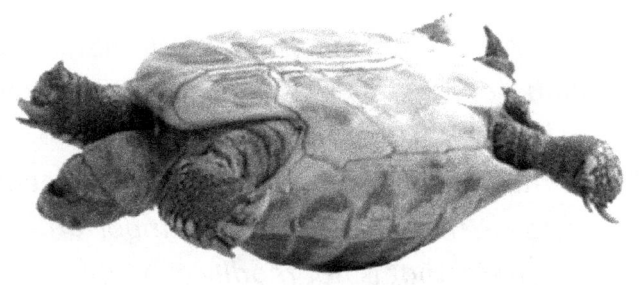

So, when you find yourself on your back, feeling overwhelmed, take a deep breath, summon your inner strength, and with a decisive push, turn yourself back over again. You can find the strength within to turn adversity into opportunity.

But remember, turtles cannot remain on their back, the weight on top of their lungs will eventually suffocate them, so sometimes they may need help. Sometimes, if they can't flip themselves over, maybe you could offer a little help. Each time you flip yourself back onto your feet, you grow stronger and more steadfast, ready to face the challenges of life with renewed vigor and hope. And if someone helps you every once in a while, thank them, and move forward.

WAVES ON THE BEACH

Imagine a sun-drenched beach where the rhythmic lull of the waves serenade you into a state of relaxation. Now, imagine the turtle gliding effortlessly through these same gentle waves.

The turtle understands the value of relaxation, of finding peace amid the relentless motion of the sea. Bask in the warmth of the sun. Bury your toes in the cool sand. Think about the grace of the sea turtle gliding through the cool ocean waters.

Imagine yourself swimming with them, exploring coral reefs, sunken pirate ships and hidden caves. Let the feelings wash over you like the waves that will wash over the beach removing the footprints of those who stepped on it just a few moments earlier. Once your beach is smooth again, you can take another first step into your daily journey.

JUST KEEP SWIMMING

The baby sea turtle never stops swimming once they hit the ocean's waves. Like them, you should never stop swimming towards your goals in life. Yes, you may get tired. Yes, you may need to dodge predators and take detours in your life... but those detours should only temporarily lead you astray. Eventually, you will navigate your way back onto your proper path.

From there, just keep swimming!

TRUST ME, YOU WILL GROW QUICK!

Turtles may start life as tiny hatchlings, but they grow and mature very quickly. Similarly, humans start small and vulnerable, undergo rapid and transformative growth, evolving into individuals with boundless potential.

Each stage of life is a period of intense learning, adaptation, and growth. The turtle rapidly acquires the skills and strength needed to survive and thrive, but humans undergo significant transformations. It takes years to acquire the knowledge, skills, and wisdom we need.

Both turtles and humans share a common truth: the journey from small beginnings to full maturity is a process of rapid and profound change.

OCEAN PUNS

Homonyms make the best puns – specifically in the written word. Homonyms are words that have the same spelling or pronunciation but different meanings. Examples include:

> "Maid" (house cleaner) and
> "made" (past tense of make).

> "There" (location),
> "their" (possessive), and
> "they're" (contraction of they and are)

Puns treat homonyms as synonyms. A synonym is a word or phrase that has the same meaning as another word. One example is:

> "The wedding was so emotional
> that even the cake was in tiers."

I'm a Dad Joke kind of girl that absolutely loves the written word. Puns are one of the biggest word tricks in the bag, and I love using these in hopes of putting a smile on somebody's face. Enjoy!

SEAS THE DAY

Each day for a turtle is an opportunity to explore new territories, to glide with the currents, and to embrace the rhythm of the waves. The turtle's journey is a testament to living fully and purposefully.

You should choose to seize the day just like a turtle. Explore the world full of luscious landscapes, endless possibilities and where the sky is the limit.

Each wave offers a new chance to move forward, each day a fresh opportunity to make the most of our time here on earth.

By living with intention and seizing the day, we align ourselves with the turtle's graceful journey, making every moment count in our own adventure through life's boundless sea.

BE SHORE OF YOURSELF

I say it all of the time and infrequently listen to my own advice – trust your instinct! Your first thought is almost always the right thing to do. Yet, we tend to second guess our first impression. We make excuses why we should do something when we know we shouldn't.

Be sure of yourself. Being sure of yourself means embracing your strengths and trusting your instincts. It involves moving forward with the assurance that you are capable and determined, even when faced with challenges.

If you could emulate the turtle's quiet confidence and assuredness, and coast through the waters of life with your head up and neck out... If you could be shore of yourself, let life be your compass as you chart your course through the ever-changing sea of life.... You can do anything!

COME OUT OF YOUR SHELL

I am a shy person. When I am surrounded by strangers. I may not withdraw my head into my shell with a thrust backwards and a hiss, but I do tend to stand alone in a corner, taking in the scene while trying to find a way to venture into the unknown or plan my exit strategy. That being said, once I feel comfortable in my surroundings, I will come out of my shell and Wow the World!

TAKE TIME TO COAST

Sometimes life feels like a roller coaster. The day speeds by so fast you have no idea where the time went. Sometimes, you feel like you are standing still, waiting for the cars to reload. And other times you feel like you are pressed back into your seat, climbing a ladder so steep you almost fear what is on the other side.

Thus is the life of a sea turtle. They swim the narrow channels, ride the waves and get tossed around in the storms. They also dive deep into the depths of the ocean to escape the turbulence of life and seek much needed rest.

Yet, like the females who return to land to lay eggs, you must still return to the coast and watch the sun rise, as a new day and a new adventure awaits you.

AVOID PIER PRESSURE

In life, peer pressure can feel like unpredictable ocean currents, trying to push you off course or compel you to conform to others' expectations. Yet, like the turtle, you possess the power to remain steadfast and true to yourself.

Turtles trust their instincts and follow their own paths. Trust your values and make decisions that reflect who you truly are. Embrace your individuality, it is a strength, not a weakness.

When faced with external pressures, remember that maintaining control is vital. Just as turtles swim against the tide when necessary, you too can stand firm against influences that don't resonate with your beliefs. So, navigate your own course with assurance and pride. Be inspired by the turtle's grace and courage, and let your unique voice shine through the currents of life.

MAKE WAVES

In life, there are rules, expectations and demands. You must be on time. You must get the job done. You must not ask too many questions and you must not buck the system. Yet sometimes, making waves is a necessary survival tool.

If something doesn't seem right, or someone is rubbing you the wrong way, it is not your obligation to stay quiet, it is your duty to speak up! Make waves. Even if they are small waves.

Even the smallest waves can create the ripple effect needed to exact the change needed in the world.

Don't Get Tide Down

As an author, as an entrepreneur, as a wife and a turtle 'mom' I find the overwhelming tasks of daily life weighing me down. Sometimes I feel tied to my desk, to the house, or to the project, but that is truly all a mindset.

Unless a fishing net has snagged you, wrapped around your fins and neck and is holding you in place, you have the freedom to swim around it. You have the ability to dive below or leap out of the waters of life to escape the grasp of life's binding ropes.

You were made not to work, but to experience all that life has to offer. You may want to work, but you are not shackled to your desk. Get up, stretch your neck, wiggle your fins and breath in the freedom of a warm sunny day or a cool dip in the pond. This is your life.

SEA LIFE'S BEAUTY

Life is filled with moments of beauty and wonder, found in the most unexpected places. Take the time to appreciate the world around you; like the sea turtle. The magnificent colors of a sunrise, the sounds of tiny raindrops, or the simple joy of a shared smile.

Turtles remind us to appreciate the beauty of our environment. Each day is an exploration of the ocean's wonders. From vibrant coral reefs to the soft lapping of waves, by adopting the turtle's perspective, you can discover beauty in both grand landscapes and simple moments.

Let this appreciation guide you through life, making every day a journey of discovery and wonder. Allow yourself to pause and soak in the little things. Swim gracefully through your habitat, like a turtle. You, too, can glide through life with an open heart and a curious spirit.

Embrace the beauty, and let it inspire you to see the world with fresh eyes. Life's most precious moments often come from simply being present.

YOU ARE SHELL-DOM ALONE

I think there should be a category called Olympic turtle stacking. Pyramids of turtles, as seen in ponds on logs or small islands, remind us that socializing is a vital part of their existence.

These delightful creatures thrive in community, demonstrating that even in their individual journeys, they find strength and companionship in numbers. "Safety in numbers," Mom said.

Your journey, while uniquely yours, and sometimes seemingly done alone, is almost always accompanied by the presence of family, friends, and countless others who traverse their own paths alongside you.

Turtles come together to bask in the sun or share a space, you too could find support and joy in your connections.

Remember, you are seldom alone in life.

Embrace the relationships that enrich your life, and allow yourself to lean on others when needed. Together, you can create a beautiful tapestry of shared moments and mutual growth.

So, celebrate the connections you have, just like those turtles enjoying their time together. Life's journey is not just about reaching your destination, but also about the bonds you forge along the way.

Embrace the warmth of companionship, knowing that together, you can navigate the waters of life more gracefully.

WATER CANNOT SINK A SHIP UNLESS IT GETS INSIDE

Isn't it odd that a boat can float on water, but if that water gets inside, it can sink the ship?

Life's challenges are like the ocean's waves; powerful and persistent. But the good news is, they only pose a threat if you allow them in. If you let them penetrate your inner peace.

Equally a ship's hull is designed to keep water out, you have the power to safeguard your own well-being. You have the ability to step away, say no, or not answer the call.

When faced with difficulties, remember that your inner strength and courage are crucial. Don't let external pressures, fears, or negative influences breach your personal defenses.

Like a turtle relying on its shell for protection from the harsh elements of the sea, you too can create a barrier that shields you from life's turmoil.

Focus on what strengthens and supports you.

Surround yourself with positivity, nurture your passions, and cultivate your sense of purpose. By doing so, you can navigate the waves of life with grace and confidence, knowing that you have the power to keep the waters outside where they belong. Embrace your strength, and let your inner peace be your anchor!

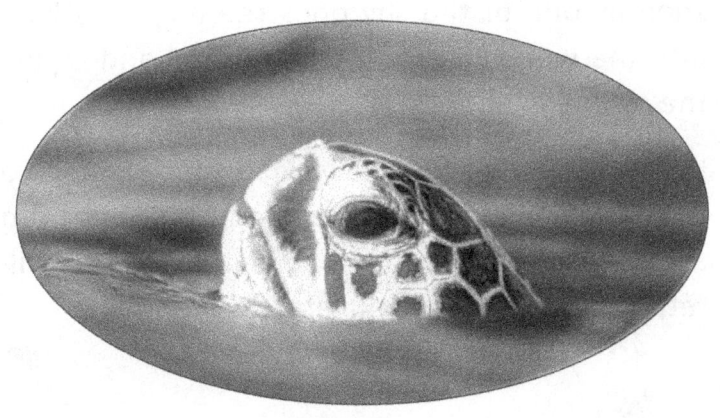

I'LL SEA YOU LATER

When I am sitting outside by my pond, I love glancing over at the turtles and watching them peek their heads out of the water to smile at me.

Yes, they are looking to see if I bring food, or if I plan on leaving them in peace to venture out on land and bask, but those are just the shy ones. I have much more social turtles who don't mind my being there at all. I guess then, it takes all kinds to make up a pond.

Sometimes I step outside and see six or seven turtles piled up in their crazy pyramids and as soon as one of the shy ones see me, they leap into the water, toppling the pyramid and taking the others with them.

It's okay. You never know what life is going to throw at you or what it's going to pull out from under you. All I know is eventually they will return, and I will sea you later.

SOAK UP THE SUNLIGHT

SUNRISES OF HOPE SUNSETS OF PEACE

In the world you will find light and darkness. But the good book teaches us one very important thing... there cannot be darkness without light.

When you are feeling lost in darkness, or the shadows are starting to envelop your being, simply shine the light of hope on it and it will wipe out the darkness.

No matter how dark the night may become, there will always be a sunrise. Take that to heart. And no matter how hard you fought that day in the light, there will always come a sunset so you can seek rest. This is why you should embrace both sides of this coin. It is not here to swallow you whole, it is here to teach you the value of life.

> **May every sunrise bring you hope
> and every sunset bring you peace.**

YOUR SMALL LIGHT CAN MAKE A BIG DIFFERENCE

If you are young, maybe you feel that you are not wise beyond your years. If you are a small person, maybe you feel like you cannot be big and bold just yet. If you are shy, maybe you feel like your voice cannot be heard. And if you haven't a degree, maybe you feel like your knowledge isn't enough. Whatever it is that is holding you back from expressing yourself, your thoughts or your ambitions, stop thinking this way now.

You may think your light is small, but it can make a big difference in others. Have you ever turned on a light that has a dimmer and at the lowest setting the room seems way too dark to do you any good? Well, if you wait for your eyes to adjust, taking in what little light there is and amplifying it for your benefit, it works.

Give it time. You will get there.

EVERY SUNRISE IS A CHANCE AT A NEW BEGINNING

Every sunrise is a chance at a new beginning. Now, envision the turtle as it rises with the morning sun, its tiny form silhouetted against the emerging light. Each dawn offers a fresh canvas, a moment to start anew and embrace the limitless potential of the day ahead.

The sunrise symbolizes renewal, illuminating the path forward and encouraging us to leave behind yesterday's worries. Just as the turtle sets out with a renewed sense of purpose each morning, we too can approach each day with the same.

Let the beauty of each sunrise remind you that every moment is an opportunity to grow, explore, and redefine your journey.

Embrace the promise of a new day, knowing that you have the power to shape your own story. With each sunrise, rise with intention, and make the most of the possibilities that await you!

LET IT WARM YOU INSIDE OUT

Let it warm you inside out. Even as turtles bask in the sun, allowing its rays to warm their shells, you too can embrace the sun's warmth to bring comfort and rejuvenation to your spirit.

Imagine a turtle, stretched out on a sunlit rock, soaking in the light. As the sunlight touches its shell, it not only warms its body but also invigorates its very essence.

In the same way, allow the sun's warmth to fill you completely. Let it warm your heart and mind, infusing you with a sense of peace and vitality.

Take a moment to step outside, feel the sun on your skin, and let it remind you of life's simple pleasures. Likewise, the turtle finds solace in the sun's embrace, you can find renewal and strength in the warmth of each day.

Allow this radiant energy to inspire you, rejuvenate your spirit, and empower you to navigate life with grace and confidence.

**Embrace the warmth,
and let it illuminate your path!**

SPEND TIME AT THE BEACH

Spending time at the beach can have a positive impact on your physical and mental health. It offers a unique environment where the visual of flowing water, the sound of the waves crashing, the smell of the salty sea air, all combine giving your senses a rush.

Going to the beach can be quite refreshing but some of us just don't live near one or can't find the time to get away. Well, they make videos of the sights. Audio of the sounds. Fans for the breeze and sunshine for the rays. With your eyes closed and your creativity enhanced, or even just a little imagination, you can find a way to escape.

But if you can get there.... Watch and listen to the sea guls crying out as they soar above the waters. Feel the cool wet sand between your toes as it invigorates your senses. Get wet. Sit and watch a sunset. Meditate to the sound of the waves washing up on shore. Explore the environment as you hunt for sea shells or play with sand castles.

Unlike sea turtles, who only return to the beach they were born on to lay their eggs, you can gain way more stress relief and go back any time you want to. Enjoy a day at the beach. Take it all in. Let it wash over you, and then go home relaxed, invigorated and ready to face a new day.

WATCH FOR THE SUN SETS

Out here in the Texas hill country we get some fantastic sunsets! Clouds of all shapes and sizes decorate a red, orange, pink or purple sky giving the impression of distance that can make the eyes goggle for long moments of pure joy.

There have been times that I was driving over hills and saw what was an optical illusion of clouds and sky that looked like a distant ocean just ahead, or purplish-blue mountains surrounding a bright blue lake. The visuals are enough to make you lose sight of where you are going.

Don't lose focus for long though. You must revert your eyes back to the road so you can get home safely. You don't want to fall from your path.

In a world full of things that can divert your attention from your intended goal in life, try to remember to return your focus on your path.

Sure, you can navigate down an alternate path for a while. You can escape down a terrific trail or a rising road, but eventually, you must shift your steering to the street.

Watch for sunsets but also watch the street. And if you can't do both at the same time, pull over for a moment and take in that beautiful sight.

Seeing the beauty of the world and what God has to gift you is a journey in of itself.

JUST ENOUGH CLOUDS FOR A GLORIOUS SUNSET

Imagine the evening sky adorned with a gentle scattering of clouds, allowing the setting sun to paint the heavens with brilliant hues of gold, pink, reds, and purple. This harmonious interplay between light and shadow creates a spectacle that is both awe-inspiring and tranquil, a beautiful reminder of God and nature's artistry.

Now imagine a sea turtle navigating through cold, murky waters, resolved to reach that sunlit shore. A resolve to face the second most challenging moment in their lives. To lay a hundred plus eggs after a thousand-mile swim.

If they can do that, we can embrace the clouds in our lives. Each challenge, each moment of uncertainty, adds depth to our journey, enhancing the richness and splendor of our personal sunset.

Let each cloud contribute to your unique experience. Embrace the sunsets, for they highlight the brilliance of your achievements and the beauty of your growth.

May you find joy in every color of your journey. Celebrate the intricate blend of light and darkness that shapes your life. Remember, it's the interplay of these elements that creates a truly glorious sunset!

DARKNESS CAN'T LAST WHEN YOU SHINE YOUR LIGHT

Darkness can't last when you shine your light on it. So, when a turtle navigates through murky waters, it embodies an inner resolve that drives it forward, breaking through the depths where light is scarce and emerging on the other side, wide-eyes and open-finned.

Your inner light, like the turtle's steadfast journey, has the capacity to pierce through even the most enveloping shadows.

In life, we all encounter dark moments, but remember: you possess the power to illuminate your path. Just as the turtle persists, steadily moving toward the surface, let your light shine brightly, even in the darkest of times.

Embrace your inner strength, allowing it to guide you through the shadows. With every step you take, you challenge the darkness, proving that it cannot endure when met with the brilliance of your hope and tenacity.

So, like the turtle emerging from the deep water to bask in the sun, trust in your ability to rise above adversity. Your light is a beacon, a testament to your journey, and a reminder that even the darkest night will give way to a brighter dawn. Shine on!

IT IS ONLY IN THE LIGHT THAT YOU CAN SEE

Imagine the turtle emerging from the depths of the ocean and gliding into the sunlit shallows. In this warm and clear environment, the turtle can appreciate the vibrant colors of coral reefs, the shifting patterns of sand, and the graceful movements of other sea creatures. The light transforms its surroundings from a shadowy expanse into a vivid landscape full of wonder.

In life, light symbolizes understanding, clarity, and insight. When you immerse yourself in the light, whether through knowledge, self-awareness, or moments of inspiration, you gain the ability to see things more clearly.

Challenges and obstacles become easier to navigate, and you can fully appreciate the richness of your experiences.

Just like the turtle relies on light to guide its journey and reveal the ocean's treasures, you too can benefit from seeking clarity in your own life.

Embrace the moments of illumination, allowing them to shine a path forward. Remember, it is in the light that you can truly see, understand, and thrive. Let it guide you toward the beauty and possibilities that await you!

Don't Let Yourself Get Burned

Contrary to public belief turtles can indeed get sunburned! Their shells may protect them, but the thin skin on their feet, tail and head can definitely burn with too much exposure to the sun. Yes, they love to bask, and unlike you, who can wear sunscreen, they must return to the waters before the sun exposure becomes too much. But that is not the only way you can get burned in life.

You can get burnout from emotional, mental or physical exhaustion brought on by repeated stresses. You can also get burned by a bad deal gone wrong or someone who is thoughtless.

It is important to be aware of the situations around you and when necessary, escape into those cool waters to refresh your perspective.

SWIM WITH THE TIDE

SWIM WITH THE CURRENT

While I do encourage you to step out of the ocean and take a journey, I also want to encourage you to swim with the current. Yes, that sounds contradictory, but hear me out. Life is about the journey. It is a long one. Each day is a new adventure. Each opportunity is a new experience. Each person you meet has the potential to build your character or enhance your being. So try it all. Swim with the current as well as bask in the sun. You can do something new each day.

GET IN THE WATER

If you want to learn how to swim, you must first get in the water. Turtles begin their journey in the water, navigating their surroundings with grace and curiosity. Just like turtles, which instinctively dive into their aquatic homes, you too must take that leap to embrace new experiences.

In life, growth often requires stepping out of your comfort zone. When you immerse yourself in new challenges, you not only learn essential skills but also discover your own resilience. Like the turtle exploring the deep waters, allow yourself to embrace the unknown and trust in your ability to adapt and thrive. So, don't hesitate, dive in!

Whether it's learning a new skill, facing your fears, or pursuing your dreams, remember that every great swimmer started with a single splash. Let the water guide you to new horizons!

SWIM AT YOUR OWN PACE

Picture the turtle gliding through the sea, its movements unhurried yet purposeful.

It doesn't rush or compare itself to the swift currents or other sea creatures. Instead, it maintains its own steady rhythm, trusting in its strength and following its unique path.

This approach allows it to traverse the immense ocean with courage and confidence.

Similarly, in life, it's vital to honor your own rhythm and progress. Each person's journey is unique, and the pace at which you move is as individual as you are.

The turtle doesn't need to keep up with the fast-moving currents or the fleeting fish. You don't have to match the pace of others either. Focus on your own growth and milestones.

Embrace the wisdom of the turtle by navigating through life at a pace that feels right for you.

Allow yourself the time and space to grow, learn, and achieve your goals without undue pressure. Remember, it's not about how fast you swim, but about the journey itself and the beauty of moving forward at your own pace.

**Trust in your journey,
and let your unique rhythm guide you!**

WATER MAKES YOU WEIGHTLESS

Imagine a freshwater turtle gracefully gliding through the water, experiencing the sensation of weightlessness as it moves so effortlessly. This profound feeling offers a powerful metaphor for how we can find moments of release and tranquility in our own lives.

In these serene moments, like the turtle floating free, you are not held back by the weight of stress or responsibilities. Instead, you find yourself in a state of ease and calm, where the burdens of the world seem to dissipate.

A swimming turtle seems weightless. You too can embrace these times of weightlessness as opportunities to rejuvenate and gain perspective.

Allow yourself to seek out and savor these moments of freedom. Whether through meditation, spending time in nature, or simply taking a quiet moment to breathe.

These experiences can help you rise above the pressures of daily life. Remember, like the turtle, you have the ability to float, to let it all go, and to rediscover your inner peace.

Embrace the weightlessness, and let it lift you to a deeper understanding of yourself and your ultimate journey!

LEARN TO SURF THE WAVES

The world is spinning at a brisk 1000 miles per hour. Granted, the earth is round so that number changes the closer you get to the poles, but for the purpose of this demonstration we will go with the speed. We are spinning fast and the currents it causes and the waves it creates can be great!

And for the purpose of this message, simply put, you cannot stop the waves. If you are going to emerge to the surface, nearing the beach, then you must be prepared to either surf the waves or get swept under. So learn how to surf!

Find your balance. Align your sight to the horizon. Step onto the surfboard of life and hang ten. You can't stop the waves but you can learn to surf them.

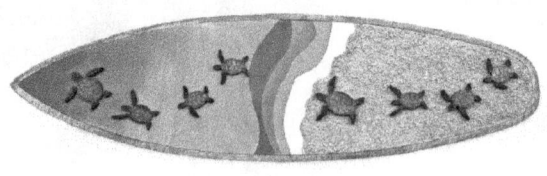

A GOOD NAVIGATOR

Navigating through life's journey can sometimes be difficult for a turtle. From sea turtles who are born on a beach, navigating to the oceans waves is fraught full of obstacles. From predators trying to pick them off from the sky, sand as well as in the sea. Sea turtle hatchlings face danger from the moment they are born.

Likewise, female land turtles come out of the water to navigate dry land in order to lay their eggs. Many of them travel long distances and even cross roads to get there. Predators are still a concern as they lay their eggs and then on the long trek home, as they cross the same roads going back. These are just the dangers of life.

But if you are a good navigator, you look both ways, you stay focused on your task, and you are aware of your surroundings, you will get there (and home) eventually.

The Well-Traveled Turtle

Sea turtles travel great distances. The ocean is huge and there is a lot to see and do. There are a ton of sea creatures to meet or to hide from, and there are a lot of sites to see.

They travel south to find warm waters, they travel north when cold waters turn warm, and they travel back to the land with which they were born on, to lay eggs of the next generation of turtles.

From their very first day of life, they are looking forward to their travels.

They do not know where the ocean is going to take them, but it is always going to be a wild, adventurous ride. Travel often.

WHEN YOU TIRE, REACH FOR THE EDGE

If you have ever spent time in the water, maybe the deep end of the pool, maybe the tidal pool at an amusement park, maybe a lake, or ocean, you will find yourself growing tired the longer you wade the deep waters

So when you find yourself tiring out, and you seek some rest, reach for the edge of the pool, step out onto the beach and find a few moments to catch your breath, to experience the rest you need.

TURTLE FLIPPERS DON'T WRINKLE

The longer you wade in the water, the wrinklier your fingers get. Pruny, is what Mom called them, and that was a sign you needed to get out, dry off, warm up and get something to drink.

But turtle flippers don't wrinkle. They stay the same no matter how long a turtle stays in the water. And yet, they still climb out of the water to bask, warm up and dry out every once in a while, and their Mom didn't have to tell them that, they just instinctively knew it.

I don't know how we know when to retreat to dryland or when to dive back into the water, we just do, and so do you. You know what roads you should travel in life.

Your instinct tells you what is right and what is wrong. You may second guess yourself, but that is just an excuse to stay in the water longer than you should. Get out before you get pruney.

A WATER-LOGGED LESSON

A storm is brewing. The rain is pouring down. The wind is causing waves to crash against the shore. The downpour is enough to make us feel weighed down and waterlogged, but the storm does not define our journey.

In moments of hardship, it may feel like we're sinking under the weight of it all, but the turtle shows us that we can endure. We can eventually find calmer waters, too.

Sunshine emerges after the rain. The weight of the world feels lighter, a brighter day is waiting for you. Your shell may feel waterlogged now, but in time, the burden will ease. The storm will pass, and you will emerge stronger, wiser, and ready to continue your journey.

IT'S ALL ABOUT THE CLIMB

LIFE IS A CLIMB, BUT THE VIEW IS GREAT

I watch movies, tv shows and documentaries of mountain climbers traversing up a mountain and all of the challenges they face. They must carry everything they need, on their back, like a turtle, including their tent/shelter.

They feel the challenges as they gain new heights as the gravity becomes stronger and the air becomes thinner. They get light headed, wear out faster and the cold – don't even get me started on the terrifying temperatures they endure trying to reach their goals.

Watching them is absolutely exhausting to me, and I am just sitting on the couch. That being said though, when they reach the top, and they look out at the world around them. They see the horizon so far off in the distance and they rejoice their triumphant success, I do, kind of want to see it for myself. Maybe one day I will?

The Best View Often Comes After the Hardest Climb

Turtles carry their homes on their backs,
a constant reminder of their strength.

Can you imagine the weight of that load as they navigate land, water, and everything in between? While it keeps them grounded, it also teaches us that there's nothing wrong with staying in our comfort zones (a place I really like to be).

Yet, every so often, a spark ignites within us, urging us to reach new heights and explore uncharted territories. Step out of our comfort zones and try something new.

Sometimes, the hardest climbs are the ones we must undertake. But the effort is worth it. When you finally reach the summit and gaze out at the world before you, the beauty will envelop you and warm your soul in ways you never expected.

It's in those moments of triumph that you realize the journey, burdened as it may have been, has shaped you into who you are.

So embrace the climb, carry your load with pride, and allow the view from the top to inspire you for the next adventure!

And if you don't reach the top on your first try, each new day gives you an opportunity to try again. So take that climb. You will reach it.

CLIMB MOUNTAINS, NOT SO THE WORLD CAN SEE YOU, BUT SO YOU CAN SEE THE WORLD

When water turtles in captivity find a log, a wall, or a stack of rocks, they eagerly climb to reach new heights. Watching them stretch their limbs and bask at the top, eyes closed and faces turned toward the sun, is a reminder of the peace that comes with reaching for our dreams.

But those turtles aren't climbing for our benefit, they are seeking a broader view of the world around them and the benefits of spending time soaking up the sun.

In your own life, don't feel pressured to scale the tallest mountains simply to meet the expectations of others. Instead, climb for yourself. The true reward comes from gaining a new perspective and discovering your potential. If others appreciate your journey along the way, that's a wonderful bonus, but it shouldn't be your sole motivation in life. This is about you!

So, climb those mountains. Not to be seen, but to see the world. Embrace your own path, and find joy in the heights you achieve for your own sake. Your journey is yours alone, and every summit brings you closer to the life you envisioned for yourself.

BEING ON THE BOTTOM IS THE FIRST STEP TOWARDS SUCCESS

Turtle pyramids are one of the most fascinating sights to behold. Aquatic turtles, being cold-blooded, need to bask in the sun to warm up, and when space is limited, they get creative.

One turtle climbs out onto a sun-drenched spot, and soon another follows. If there's no room for a third, that turtle simply climbs on top of the first two, forming a delightful pyramid that keeps growing until the turtle on top decides to take a plunge back into the water (or the one on the bottom who takes everyone with him.)

This cycle of climbing and diving is a beautiful metaphor for our own journeys. Each turtle gets a chance to bask in the sun, taking turns as we all seek our moments of success. But sometimes, when one turtle on the bottom slips back into the water, the pyramid topples. Yet this doesn't signify failure; it's just a new beginning.

The bottom turtle's descent opens the door for someone else to rise. Remember, being at the bottom is often the first step toward success. It's where growth happens, where lessons are learned, and where new opportunities arise.

So embrace your journey, knowing that every climb leads to new possibilities!

WHEN YOU REACH THE TOP, KEEP CLIMBING

One of the coolest things about turtles, especially aquatic ones, is how they can bask at the highest point in their pond, soaking up the sun for as long as they like. But eventually, they dive back into the water to explore new depths. Just like mountain climbers who seek to conquer various peaks, reaching the top doesn't mean the journey is over, it's just the beginning of another new adventure. Each day offers a fresh opportunity to set new goals and tackle new challenges.

So, whether you're climbing mountains or diving into the unknown, remember that growth comes from embracing the journey. Don't settle for one peak; keep exploring and expanding your horizons. Every climb leads to new experiences, and each dive reveals hidden treasures.

**So go on, keep moving forward,
your next adventure awaits!**

SET A GOAL, THEN REACH FOR IT

You can do anything you set your mind to. I know you've heard that before, but it's the truth. What do you want to do in life? What do you want to do today? Yes, you may have responsibilities, but you CAN take a few moments for yourself. Even if it is a small goal, set one, then reach for it. I'll tell you one thing, if I didn't reach for my goals, even little goals, this book wouldn't exist.

CLIMBING IS AS CLOSE AS WE CAN COME TO FLYING

Yes, I know humans have built airplanes, hang gliders, parachutes and even rocket packs, so they can fly, but a turtle doesn't have the opposable thumbs or access to the technology to invent things like that. So when I write that climbing is as close as we can come to flying, I am looking at it from a turtles perspective.

Have you ever seen a turtle climb a fence? Straight up! Traversing upwards like he was climbing a ladder. Think it is rare, think again.

I watched one of my own turtles climb our drapes to get to the top of our couch. Scared the heck out of me when I caught something large moving to the side of my head with my peripheral vision!

The point I am trying to make, albeit in a very roundabout way, is, when you climb you reach new heights, and as you look out at the colossal world around you, even if it is just the top of the couch, you can not only see how much farther you have to go, but you can also see where you were. Where you came from.

As you look out, it can almost feel like you are flying. Taking sail into a brand-new door, a new opportunity, awaiting our next great leap of faith.

THE TURTLE ONLY MAKES PROGRESS WHEN IT STICKS ITS NECK OUT

One of the coolest things about turtles is their ability to retract their necks into their shells, like finding refuge from the blazing sun or hiding from larger predators.

For box turtles, their hinged shells allow them to close up completely, almost like shutting the door to keep the cool air in. But while staying tucked away feels safe, it can also keep you from moving forward. True growth happens when you take that leap; when you stick your neck out and step outside of your comfort zone.

That's my favorite turtle joke, as well... What make a turtle such a good friend? They stick their neck out for you. I know it's hokey, but it is 100% me!

It's in those moments of vulnerability, whether by lending a hand to someone in need or exploring the unknown, that life truly begins to unfold around us.

So, embrace the adventure! Offer your help, take a chance, and step into the world. Only then will you discover new paths and make meaningful progress. Remember, just like our turtle friends, it's the moments we venture out that lead to the greatest experiences.

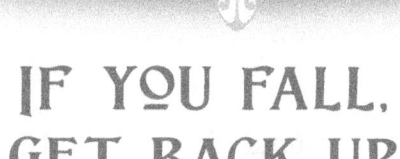

IF YOU FALL, GET BACK UP

Turtles climb. They climb tree limbs, river banks, rocks and even fences. Nothing will stop them from getting to their intended destination—except maybe gravity.

When I see a turtle fall, either from a ramp, rock or limb, I immediately go to them to help them. They are my pets in captivity and that is my duty. But what about those out in the wild, who don't have a larger being overseeing their care?

Well, they still have to get back up. They have to flip themselves back over or they will perish. I won't go into the problems if they stay on their back for too long, but I will say, you have to push yourself hard, no matter how hard it seems.

If there isn't someone around to help you, making the experience easier, survival will only make you stronger. Get back up if you fall.

WHEN YOU REACH THE TOP

Look for higher mountains to climb. Why not? Most of the time, when a turtle climbs to its highest peak, it loves to stretch its neck out, see what is out there and then make a plan. Before long, it will dive back into the waters, swim to the next obstacle and then set forth to climb it. One day, who knows, maybe there will be mountain turtle as prolific as sea turtles. If you can imagine it, you can do it.

Relax & Slow Down

TAKE TURTLE TIME FOR YOURSELF

In our fast-paced world, it's easy to get caught up in the rush, constantly moving from one task to the next, with little time to pause and just *be*. But the turtle shows us the power of taking time for ourselves. The turtle isn't in a hurry; it knows that the journey is just as important as the destination.

Sometimes, the most valuable thing we can do is slow down and take what I like to call: ***Turtle Time.*** Take a moment to step back, breathe deep, and simply exist in the present. Whether it's sitting quietly in nature, enjoying a peaceful meal, or taking time to reflect on your day, turtle time is about honoring your own need for rest and rejuvenation. Trust that by allowing yourself moments of stillness, you'll return to your life with renewed energy, perspective, and clarity.

Give yourself the gift of Turtle Time!

Those Who Say Turtles Are Slow, Don't Know

The Tortoise and the Hare, was an insightful, encouraging story with a moral for you to keep going, no matter how slow, as you will eventually make it to the finish line, and in this story, win the race. The character choice in the story, however, created generations of biased thought towards turtles being slow. Oy-vey!

"Slow and steady wins the race."

Anyone who says turtles are slow obviously doesn't know a turtle. Turtles can be quite quick when they decide to, and their speed can baffle anyone who hasn't seen it. From crossing a hot road quickly to save their burning feet, to greeting their favorite person carrying their favorite meal when they approach.

There is even a turtle who has discovered the joys of riding a little toy skateboard, and boy can he zoom across the floor! You may always be on the go, speeding through life at a million miles per hour, but you should at least remember to slow down when you get to the other side of the road, so you can appreciate the journey.

Like a turtle racing up to see you, at least my turtles, they stop for a good back rub, shaking their shelled butts side to side in a happy dance of feel-good massage and a "hi ma, so good of you to see me."

Turtles have such neat personalities!

Relax and Unwind

I often wonder what it is like for a sea turtle in the ocean during a hurricane. I'm certain they dive deep and steer clear of the surface but they do have to emerge in order to breathe. What do they do then? They remain still and wait it out.

Life has a way of throwing us into a whirlwind, much like clothes in a spin cycle. We get tangled up in tasks, responsibilities, worries, and expectations, spinning faster and faster until we feel knotted and out of control. It's easy to get caught in the cycle of stress, trying to juggle everything at once, feeling like we're constantly in motion but getting nowhere.

The world can feel chaotic, but we have the power to stop and take a breath, to pause the cycle and allow ourselves space to rest.

GOING SLOW IS STILL PROGRESS

Sometimes it feels like the world is speeding by, racing ahead of you, leaving you behind in a whirlwind of dust. With so much happening around you, it's easy to feel stagnant, as if you're not moving at all. Progress can feel agonizingly slow, and you might begin to wonder if you'll ever truly catch up.

Just remember, you are not in a race. Your journey is uniquely yours, and it's perfectly okay to move at your own pace, just like a turtle. Each step you take, no matter how small, is still a step forward. As long as you don't give up, you will reach your goals in your own time.

So embrace your journey, savor each moment, and celebrate your progress, because no matter how slow you go, progress is progress.

Relax, Recharge and Reflect

The turtle knows that life's currents may be strong, but it doesn't rush against them. Instead, it takes time to bask in the sun, to dive beneath the surface, and to recharge its energy. It knows the value of stillness, of reflection, and of taking the time to replenish.

In our busy lives, we often forget the importance of pausing. But like the turtle rests in the waters of life, we too must allow ourselves moments of quiet to restore our spirit. The world moves fast, but true clarity and peace come when we take the time to reflect on our journey, to reconnect with ourselves, and gather strength for the path ahead.

Life doesn't always have to be a race. Sometimes, the most powerful thing you can do is float, rest, and let the waters of life carry you for a while.

STRETCH YOUR APPENDAGES

There's something magical about watching turtles basking on a log, their limbs outstretched as if they're soaring through the sky. Who knows? Maybe they dream of flying!

Just like those turtles, we can embrace the joy of stretching and reaching for the skies. Take a moment to raise your arms high, feeling the warmth of the sun on your skin. Extend your fingertips as if trying to touch the clouds above. Then, find a comfortable seat and stretch your legs out, pointing your toes and feeling every muscle awaken.

This simple practice not only energizes your spirit but also gets the blood flowing and revitalizes your body. Remember, just like our turtle friends, stretching is a way to connect with your surroundings and embrace the freedom to explore. So, stretch, breathe, and let yourself fly… if only for a moment.

The Butt-Breather

The Fitzroy River Turtle of Australia is able to extract oxygen from water through its cloaca (through its behind) as a method of respiration to obtain as much as two-thirds of its oxygen supply. It does so by pumping water in and out of its rear end, absorbing oxygen from the water, which allows it to stay underwater for extended periods of time and even hibernate there.

Since the human body is incapable of performing such a task, and I personally am very glad about that, it is important for you to note that you shouldn't be a butt-breather.

JUST BREATHE

Aquatic turtles can spend hours submerged under water without coming up for air. Like them, we too need moments of stillness. These creatures often hold their breath while they rest, conserving energy and embracing the calm. But remember, the more we engage with the world, the more we need to rise for a breath of fresh air.

While the unique Australian Fitzroy (butt-breathing) River turtle can extract oxygen from water through its cloaca (butt), most of us need to surface every now and then so we can take a moment to breathe deeply and reconnect to the world around us.

So, take a moment for yourself. Inhale the possibilities and exhale the stress. Just breathe. It will invigorate your spirit and remind you of the beauty in both stillness and movement.

SLOW DOWN, LIFE IS NOT A RACE

Children are always in a hurry to grow up. It's a race to get to adulthood so that way they can go out into the world and do whatever they want to.

I remember thinking to myself, I cannot wait until I get to start MY life! I'll do everything MY way. And I kept thinking that into my 20's while learning my trade. My 30's while working to save up money to buy a house. My 40's until I can retire and enjoy this beautiful world God gave us... I hadn't realized life had already started and the best time, was happening now.

So slow down! Be like a turtle. Appreciate each moment of each day. Because, between you and me, rushing to adulthood is not really what you want to do in life. Being an adult is hard. You have to work, pay bills, clean house and it never stops.

LIFE CAN BE CALM AND STILL, OR ROUGH AND RIGID

Sometimes I have days and weeks that are completely uneventful. Work is mundane, no challenges. Weekends are spent on the couch because there are no book shows or ranch work needing to be done. Life is calm and still and I find myself not appreciating the break.

Other times my work day or week is booming. A project is challenging me to my core. Tech issues are making me pull my hair out, And the house work is overflowing. I look back and wonder if it will ever be calm again.

Try to appreciate the calmness, accept the rough times, and be aware it goes in cycles. Life can be calm and still or rough and rigid, but it's always beautiful. The storms of life are temporary.

SLEEP RESTORES YOUR SOUL

A BOUT OF COLD CAN SLOW YOU DOWN

Turtles are cold-blooded. This means they have a variable body temperature that is usually only slightly higher than the environmental temperature. So when the temperature outside drops down, their bodies tend to slow down. Their heartbeat slows, their breathing slows, they eventually hibernate if it gets cold enough.

I say it all of the time during the winter, I am like a turtle, if it's cold I want to hibernate. (I will never be a snow skier).

Maybe you like the cold, and that is great, but the point is, if you can cool off and slow down, that would be good to replenish your soul.

HIBERNATION IS GOOD FOR THE MIND

Meditation is a practice that involves focusing or clearing your mind using a combination of mental and physical techniques.

Depending on the type of meditation you choose, you can meditate to relax, reduce anxiety, stress, and more. On the outside, someone who's meditating might not seem to be doing anything other than breathing. Inside their brain, however, it's an entirely different story. Meditation can positively affect your brain and mental health.

While turtles won't be found sitting up on their shell, legs crossed with their flippers together, vocalizing a low humm, they do meditate. They do sun bathe with their legs and neck stretched out and absorb the sun shining down on them.

Maybe you should try.

EVERYONE AND EVERYTHING NEED SEASONS OF REST

In the stillness of winter, when everything seems quiet and dormant, there is wisdom to be found.

The trees, though bare, are gathering strength for the spring to come. The turtles, deep in their hibernation, are recharging for the adventures of warmer days. Even the cold, silent breeze carries with it a subtle reminder to prepare for growth.

In times of quiet, when our energy feels depleted or our spirits tired, we are not failing, we are simply in a season of restoration. Like the trees shedding their leaves or the birds pausing their songs, we too need moments of stillness to reflect, renew, and heal.

Trust the pauses in life. When the time is right, the spring of your growth will arrive

YAWN, IT OPENS THE LUNGS

Have you ever watched a turtle stretch and yawn, opening its mouth wide as if it was yawning? It's a reminder to breath. We often forget the simple act of breathing deeply, especially when life gets busy or overwhelming. But in the quiet moments, when we feel the need to rest, we can choose to open our lungs as the turtle opens its mouth, and inhale the peace we so often overlook. Deep, full breaths refresh and restore us, just as a yawn restores energy to the turtle's tired body.

Rest Your Eyes So You Can See Clearer

I love looking over and seeing the turtles sleeping. Their eyes closed. Their face peaceful. Their bodies still. In a world that moves fast and constantly demands our attention, it's easy to overlook the simple truth: to truly see, we must first allow ourselves to rest. Our eyes tire from hours of focus, our minds and spirits can become clouded when they are stretched too thin. But when we take the time to close our eyes, to step away, to pause, we give ourselves the space to recalibrate and refocus.

So, take a moment to close your eyes, breathe deeply, and let the world fall away for just a while. When you open them again, you may find that the path forward, is within you.

SLEEP REJUVENATES THE SPIRIT

In the quiet embrace of sleep, something magical happens. The world fades, and for a brief moment, we let go of the weight of our thoughts, our responsibilities; our worries.

Sleep is more than a physical necessity; it is an act of renewal. In those moments when we close our eyes and surrender to rest, we allow our spirit to replenish itself. It is in sleep that our dreams arise, our hearts heal, and our inner energy is refreshed. Never underestimate the power of a restful night. Your spirit is being restored for a new day.

EAT WELL, YOU MAY NEED THE NOURISHMENT

In our turtle pond at feeding time, it reminds me of the childhood game, Hungry, Hungry Hippos. I always thought they missed a perfect marketing opportunity since turtles can stretch their necks out to reach for the food and hippos do not.

For turtles they are hungry, we are too. But it is what we put in our bodies that matter. If we fed them food with no nutritional value, they would remain hungry, not grow and start to get sick. Food and its nutrients is the essence that sustains us, body and soul.

When we choose to nourish ourselves with wholesome, vibrant foods, we are not only feeding our physical bodies but also giving our spirit the energy it needs to thrive.

NOURISH YOUR SHELL

A turtle's body is its shell. To care for it, it needs vitamins, nutrients and calcium. A turtle flourishes when it receives the right care, so too do we flourish when we choose to nourish ourselves mindfully and with intention.

Eating well is a form of self-respect. It's a reminder that we deserve to feel our best, to be energized, and to honor the temple that is our body. With each meal, we are not simply filling our stomachs, we are fueling our passions, restoring our strength, and nurturing our well-being.

So, choose to nourish yourself today. Choose the foods that make you feel alive, that bring you joy, and that support the journey you are on.

ONE CANNOT REFLECT IN MOVING WATER

One cannot reflect in moving water, it must be still just like you. A turtle gliding across a pond, cannot reflect on where it has been and contemplate the future. It requires stillness.

The ripples distort the surface, and the truth beneath is hidden. But when we allow the water to settle, when we pause and allow the world around us to quiet, we can gaze deeply into its surface and see with clarity.

In a world that constantly urges us to move faster, to do more, the turtle reminds us that sometimes the most powerful thing we can do is slow down. When we quiet the noise inside and around us, we can see more clearly, think more deeply, and find the answers we've been seeking.

WIPE THE SLEEP FROM YOUR EYES

There's something peaceful about watching a turtle slowly wake up after basking in the sun for hours. I love watching them start to move and then realize their eyes are dried shut.

So they lift a front flipper and rub it along the back of its eyes, wiping away the remnants of sleep. With this simple, purposeful action, it awakens fully to the world around it.

This quiet moment is a beautiful reminder for us all. Sometimes, we wake up in life with our eyes still closed, our vision clouded by fatigue, distractions, or the weight of past thoughts. The world may be unfolding around us, but we don't see it clearly yet. Just like the turtle, we need to take a moment to "wipe the sleep from our eyes." To clear our minds, release the fog, and fully embrace the new day.

DREAM BIG

Now That's a Big Turtle!

The Giant Galápagos Tortoise can be as long as 6 feet, as wide as 3 feet, weigh as much as 880 pounds and live about 100 years!

Do Turtles Dream?

My dog dreams. He kicks in his sleep like he is running. Moans, bristles, grumbles or growls with his eyes closed. Sometimes he even cries or screams out like he's scared. I know humans dream, the majority of my stories come from my wacky dreams, but the question is, do turtles dream? I'm sure they do. Have I ever seen proof? No. But that doesn't mean they don't dream.

Everyone dreams, at some point in their lives, even if we don't remember them. I'd even go as far as to say I bet trees, plants, flowers and grass dream. Why not? I can see a tree dreaming to grow taller, grass dreaming of not getting mowed, and flowers dreaming of a bee to come by and pollinate it. We all dream. No matter what it is we dream for, we all do it, and I hope everyone's dreams come true one day.

Pursue Your Dreams

The journey toward your dreams is not always a sprint. In fact, sometimes it's more like the steady, unhurried pace of a turtle. While the world may rush ahead, the turtle moves with purpose, taking its time, trusting that every step brings it closer to its destination.

Like the turtle, you don't need to race or rush to reach your dreams. It's not about how fast you move, but about staying true to your path, one small step at a time.

Your dreams, like a distant shore, may seem far away at times, but with each movement, no matter how slow, you ARE getting closer. Dreams come true if you have the courage to pursue them. So, pursue your dreams with the heart of a turtle: steady, focused, and unwavering.

YOU CAN DO ANYTHING IF YOU SET YOUR MIND TO IT

The Galápagos tortoise is a living testament to endurance and strength. With its massive size, slow and steady pace, and longevity, this magnificent creature teaches us that greatness isn't always about speed or immediate results; it's about perseverance, focus, and the determination to keep going, no matter how long the journey may seem.

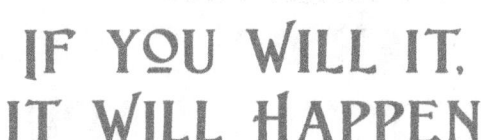

IF YOU WILL IT, IT WILL HAPPEN

You have within you the power to achieve anything you set your mind to. The road ahead may feel long and sometimes uncertain, but the key is to remain steady, to trust in your own strength, and to keep moving forward. Whether the challenges ahead are many or few, you are capable of achieving what you've set your sights on, as long as you stay true to your purpose and persist like the turtle.

Remember: It's not the fastest or the loudest who make the biggest impact, it's the ones who keep going, who keep pushing through, who sets a goal and wills it to happen.

When the world feels still and the progress seems slow, persist. If you will it, it will happen.

STRIVE TO MAKE DREAMS COME TRUE

Dreams are the whispers of our soul, the visions of possibility that call us forward. Striving to make your dreams come true is not always a smooth or easy path. There will be challenges, moments of doubt, and times when the journey feels longer than expected. But remember, every step you take, no matter how small, is a step toward realizing your vision.

Think of the tortoise, who moves slowly but steadily toward its goal, undeterred by obstacles in its way. The tortoise teaches us that it's not the speed at which we travel that matters, but the persistence to keep going. You don't need to rush or compare your progress to others. What matters is that you keep striving, one step at a time, trusting that every effort brings you closer to where you want to be.

NIGHTMARES ARE STILL DREAMS

I'm not sure I have ever seen a turtle have a nightmare though I am sure they do. My dogs will run in their sleep, kick, whimper... I do wonder if turtles react like that?

Nightmares, though often unsettling, are still part of the dreamscape. They arise from our fears, our anxieties, and the shadows that lurk in our minds. Nightmares remind us of what we need to heal, what we need to confront, and what we are capable of overcoming.

Much like the dark of night, nightmares may seem overwhelming in the moment. But they are not permanent. They are fleeting. And in their wake, we have the power to choose how we respond. We can either let them paralyze us or use them as stepping stones toward greater understanding, strength, and purpose.

So, do not fear your nightmares. Embrace them as part of your journey. They are still dreams, and in the end, they are just another chapter in the story of your growth.

Nightmares are Only Dreams You Haven't Faced. By confronting them, you not only overcome fear but you create space for new dreams to emerge, dreams that are brighter, clearer, and filled with the potential for greatness.

Don't be afraid.

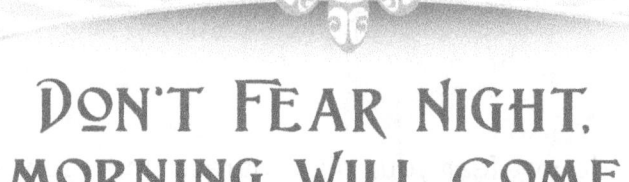

Don't Fear Night, Morning Will Come

I think to myself that it must be difficult to be a turtle. Yes, they have a shell to withdraw into, but they can't close and lock their front door, (at least not like the box turtle). They can't pull the shades and latch the windows. They sleep out there where the predators of life are, they have no real escape, it seems, sometimes.

The night may be long, and its shadows may feel heavy, but remember: no matter how dark it gets, morning always comes. The stars shine brightest against the backdrop of the night sky. Our greatest strengths often emerge in the moments when we are tested, when we are pushed to our limits.

Trust that no matter how difficult or uncertain today feels, morning will come. A new light, a new opportunity, a new beginning is always just around the corner. The night may feel long, but its purpose is to prepare you for the strength you will carry into the new day.

THE MOON MOVES THE TIDES

They say, tides are the rise and fall of sea levels caused by the combined effects of the gravitational forces exerted by the Moon as the Earth and Moon orbit one another. While it is hard to believe that the moon, some 238,855 miles away from Earth can affect the movement of Earth's oceans, it's also hard to believe that a female turtle can remember which beach she hatched on and return there to lay her eggs twenty years later.

So what stops us from believing that there may be a higher power looking out over us, moving us in powerful yet mysterious ways to complete our true reason for being here? It is important to follow our dreams, to use our talents and to share our love with this world. Maybe it's the moon moving us… or maybe it's something else. Either way, whatever it is, it is encouraging you to move!

SWIM WITH A GRACE THROUGH THE TIDES

On the land she is slow, in the water she glides, in the ocean she swims with grace through the tides." This phrase beautifully captures the journey of turtles, reflecting their adaptability and strength in various environments.

Like turtles, we each have our own rhythm.

On land, they move with deliberate slowness, reminding us that there's wisdom in taking our time and savoring each step. In the water, they glide effortlessly, symbolizing the fluidity we can find when we embrace change and flow with life's currents. And in the ocean, they swim with grace, showcasing the power of confidence as they navigate the vastness before them.

Life's journey may present us with different terrains. Some days may feel slow and heavy, while others allow us to soar with ease. Embrace your unique path, knowing that it's perfectly okay to take your time. Whether you're moving slowly on land or gracefully swimming through challenges, remember that every phase is essential to your growth.

So, like the turtle, find your balance, adapt to your surroundings, and swim through the tides of life with grace and purpose. Your journey is a beautiful dance. Embrace every moment!

NEVER GIVE UP, ONE DAY THE TIDE WILL TURN

Can you imagine being a sea turtle, exploring the enormous ocean without a road map or GPS? What if you get lost? What if you get swept downstream? What if you get washed up on shore, upside down and unable to right yourself?

Never Give Up, One Day the Tide Will Turn. When the waves wash up on shore, they will free you from your restraints and pull you back to the cool wet waters where you were meant to be.

Sometimes you may find yourself trapped or blocked, feel like a prisoner or just plain unhappy. Maybe you can dig yourself out of the sand, maybe someone will come by and help you or maybe you just need to wait until the tide comes back. Either way, the point is to not give up.

STAY OUT OF TROUBLE

TAKE THE LEAP

In the same way a turtle must choose the right moment to cross a road, we too face decisions. Trust your instincts and take the leap when the time feels right. Each turtle creates its own path, reminding us that everyone's journey is unique.

You may encounter a pothole, but see it as a chance to explore. When life throws obstacles your way, turn them into opportunities for growth and discovery.

Like the traveling turtle, don't rush. Find the road that feels true to you and navigate it cautiously.

DON'T LET LIFE STRANGLE YOU

In the sweeping oceans of life, challenges can sometimes feel like those plastic six-pack rings, tightening around your neck, making it hard to breathe. Like a turtle ensnared, you may feel trapped and overwhelmed. But remember, unlike the turtle, you can push through the struggle to break free.

Don't let life's obstacles strangle your spirit. Instead, channel your inner strength. Seek help when needed, and believe in your ability to rise above the challenges. Each struggle can teach you, shape you into a stronger, wiser version of yourself.

Maybe that wiser version will invent something as amazing as the biodegradable six pack rings made from plant-based materials, like algae or other organic substances, that break down naturally in the environment. You have the power to break free and thrive!

TANGLED UP

It's a beautiful day. The sun is shining, the ocean is calm, and the current is flowing gently. You are a sea turtle, gliding through the sapphire blue waters, soaking in the beauty around you. Schools of fish dance nearby, their shiny silver fins brushing softly against your cheeks, tickling your senses. Suddenly, a net ensnares you.

Panic surges as the fish flail, desperately trying to escape. The net tightens around you, constricting your movement. You find yourself trapped, uncertain of where you are headed or how long you can hold your breath. Thoughts race: When was the last time I surfaced for air? Do I have enough left? Should I conserve my energy?

As you are pulled to the surface, the weight of your body out of the water feels suffocating. You sense that this might be more than you can bear. Then, the net opens, and you tumble onto the deck of a boat, cushioned by a flurry of fish, though we won't dwell on their fate. Fishermen rush to your aid, working together to free you from the net. They turn you over to check for injuries, and if you're unharmed, they gently push you back into the water, releasing you not far from where you began.

This story reminds us that life can entangle us in various challenges, making us feel overwhelmed and trapped. Yet, with faith and trust, we can navigate through these difficulties and find our way back. Though we may emerge changed, stronger, braver, more cautious, and wiser, every experience helps us grow. No matter how tangled we become, we can eventually free ourselves and return to the brilliance of life.

Look Both Ways

There is an old joke that starts out, why did the turtle cross the road? Well... it may have actually been about a chicken but the topic is still the same. Especially since you see more turtles trying to cross roads than chickens these days.

While they may be crossing to get to the next water source, or seeking a safe place to lay eggs, it is important to note that the road is a dangerous place for you and for turtles. You must be aware of your surroundings.

Look both ways when crossing the road, and if you see someone in need of help getting across that road, help them to the other side, don't try to take them back to where they began.

Life is about moving forward, not being carried backwards. All you accomplish when you take a turtle back to the side they came from, is doubling their chances at getting crushed by a moving car. You see, they are going to cross that road, eventually. You cannot talk a turtle out of doing what it intends to do.

And if you are wondering why the turtle crossed the road, well one of my favorite responses to the joke is: **To get the Shell Station!**

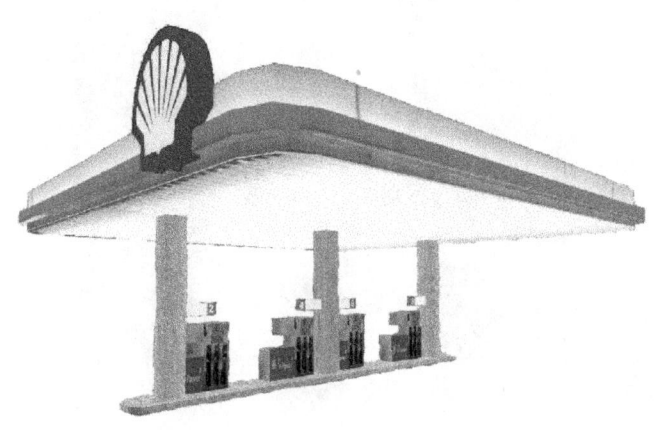

CROSSING THE ROAD

Roads are meant to be explored. Whether you are traveling down them, or walking across them, they are there and we must face them.

Like turtles crossing busy roads, we encounter unexpected challenges. Embrace these moments; they often lead to the most valuable lessons.

RESILIENCE ON THE ROAD

Turtles face obstacles on their paths, yet they persist. No matter how difficult the journey, they keep moving forward. When life's roads get tough, let the turtles tenacity inspire you to keep moving forward.

Their journey isn't fast, but it is steadfast.

You can face each challenge, learn from it, and continue your journey, just like the resilient turtle.

WHEN THE WATER DRIES UP

There are times in your life that you may feel like you are going through a dry spell. Maybe you are stuck at work, or looking for work. Maybe your creativity is gone. Maybe your love life has fizzled out. Either way, when the water dries up you have two choices, stay where you are and pray for rain, or take the first step towards a new pond or adventure. Whichever path you take is your choice and there is no right or wrong answer.

EMBRACE THE JOURNEY

Turtles may move slowly, but they savor every part of their journey. Remember, it's not just about reaching your destination, but appreciating the scenery along the way.

In a world that often prizes speed and accomplishment, the turtle reminds us that life is not a race, it is a journey to be experienced fully, step by step.

We must learn to appreciate the present moment. It's easy to become fixated on the end goal, to think that happiness and fulfillment lie only in the destination. But true peace comes when we learn to savor the scenery along the way.

So, embrace the journey. Let it be a dance of moments, of discoveries, of learning and growing.

TAKE CARE OF YOURSELF

There are no guarantees in life that you will not get hurt along the way. No matter how careful you are, no matter how much effort you spend staying out of trouble, no matter what your well-crafted plans are, sometimes things happen that you just can't control. When they do, take time to take care of yourself. Get some rest, eat well, pamper yourself and do what is good for you.

Don't Get a Big Head

There is a species of turtle called the Big-Headed Turtle and he got his name for obvious reasons. While he is unique, and rare, captured for the pet trade and hunted to near extinction, it is that big head that causes the most problems for him. When your head gets so big that you can't pull it out of danger, you put yourself in a position of vulnerability. Don't let what is a big head put you in a tough spot. Use that head for good and be smart about your choices.

THERE'S ALWAYS SOMEONE STRONGER

In the wild, turtles and tortoises navigate a world filled with challenges, knowing there are always predators bigger and stronger than they are. Yet, these resilient creatures teach us an important lesson: strength isn't just about size.

When faced with threats, turtles retreat into their protective shells, finding safety and security. This reminds us that while we may encounter obstacles or feel overshadowed by others, it's our inner strength and wisdom that truly define us.

Turtles rely on their shells for protection. We can cultivate our fortitude through self-awareness and courage. Life may present us with larger challenges or more formidable opponents, but remember that true strength lies in the ability to adapt, persevere, and seek refuge when needed. Embrace your uniqueness and trust in your abilities. Even when the odds seem stacked against you, take a page from the turtle's book: be patient, find your safe space, and don't be afraid to navigate life at your own pace.

The journey is not about being the biggest or the strongest, but about finding your way and thriving in your own right.

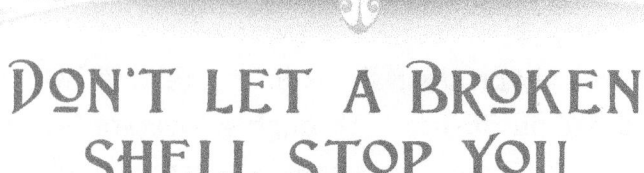

Don't Let a Broken Shell Stop You

The most heartbreaking thing to see, for me, is a turtle that had been trying to cross the road... and didn't make it. This is why I always stop when I see one still alive and help it complete its destination.

Every once in a while, I will find one that has been injured. A cracked shell or some other trauma. Even the strongest of creatures can face moments of vulnerability. The good news is, with care, time and healing, they will survive, and so will you!

Just as the shell regrows and repairs over time, we too have the ability to recover, learn, and emerge stronger than before. Life may leave scars, but those scars are not signs of weakness, they are proof of durability, growth, and endurance.

So, if you feel like your shell has been cracked or shattered, remember that healing takes time, but it is always possible.

UNIQUELY YOU

SMILE, EVEN WHEN YOU DON'T WANT TO

There's a turtle called the African Helmeted Turtle who has the most adorable little smile you've ever seen! But he's also got a bite on him that will make an Alligator Snapping turtle blush. These little guys can snag a large bird of prey and drag them to the depths of the pond to dine on. So even when you just feel like biting the head off of someone who is encroaching into your territory, just remember the African Helmet Turtles smile and let it shine.

EARN YOUR STRIPES

As a turtle born with stripes, they didn't have to earn them. What does that mean? The phrase "earn your stripes" originates from the military, where it refers to the process of earning insignia through achievements or service. It comes from the tradition of awarding stripes on a uniform to indicate rank or experience.

Each challenge we face and every milestone we reach adds a new stripe to our journey, marking our growth. Remember, it's not the speed at which we move, but the steadfastness of our progress that shapes us.

LOOK AROUND

There is a turtle called the Roti Island Snake Neck turtle. Its body is only about 7-9 inches long and its neck is about the same length.

It's neck actually looks like a small snake and if you couldn't see its shell, you would certainly think it was a snake.

They have the ability to look completely around their shells which I find fascinating, especially because it's something we should all do as well. Look around.

When you are able to see what is all around you and take it all in, the whole picture, you can make more insightful, educated decisions. Don't just see the tip of the situation because there is more to it than meets the eye.

Sometimes, there are things in life that you may miss, that without uttering a word, could tell you an entirely different story. So look around. Take it all in, and then decide how you are going to address the situation.

BLEND INTO YOUR ENVIRONMENT

There is a turtle that looks like a bunch of rotting leaves and pebbles settled on the bottom of a dirty pond. It's called the Mata Mata Turtle. The appearance of the Mata Mata's shell resembles a piece of bark, and its head resembles fallen leaves. I doubt he'll win a beauty contest.

While his camouflage is capable of hiding him quite well, until an unsuspecting fish swims by, blending into your environment is not just for staying hidden. It's designed for survival.

While it is not my place to tell you how to dress, how many piercings to get, where to place your tattoos or what color to style your hair, this world, like the Mata Mata Turtles' Pond, is designed for those who blend in properly. If you want to be taken seriously, and in the turtle's case, eat, it's best not to be the most flamboyant in the pond.

Those who are, attract the attention of predators. They can't hide in plain sight. They are seen and sometimes that is precisely what you want, and other times, it is not.

You can have your own style, and still blend into the world, just do it with moderation. And in my opinion, if you are going to add anything to your perfect body, do it in a place that can easily be hidden when you need it to be hidden.

LET YOUR SPOTS SHINE

The Spotted Turtle, with its striking yellow spots against a dark shell, is a master of camouflage, blending seamlessly into the muddy waters of bogs. Yet, when seen out on land, those vibrant spots become a beautiful focal point, catching the eye and celebrating uniqueness.

In life, we all have our own "spots." Whether they're freckles, moles, or the occasional blemish. While you may feel these features set you apart in your environment, remember that you are exactly where you're meant to be.

Embrace your unique characteristics; they are part of your story. Just like the Spotted Turtle's design serves a purpose; your spots can be seen as a testament to your individuality. Instead of hiding them, celebrate them! Find ways to appreciate what makes you unique, knowing that these qualities contribute to who you are.

Don't let anyone make you feel ashamed of your spots. Unlike turtles, we have the power to change our appearance if we wish, but it's important to love ourselves as we are.

So, whether you wash away a zit or flaunt your freckles, remember that your uniqueness is your strength. Stand proud and let your true colors shine!

YOUR EYES TELL A STORY

Did you know that eight species of box turtles have red eyes? Interestingly, most of them are male! While red eyes may not be something I'd want for myself, they remind us of the profound connection between our eyes and our emotions.

Eyes truly are the windows to the soul.

They express a range of feelings, softening in love, hardening with anger, widening in fear. They narrow in suspicion, roll in exasperation, glaze over with boredom, and well up with sadness.

Even when our mouths remain silent, our eyes can convey a smile, revealing joy and warmth or a hidden message that only someone who truly knows you can actually understand.

Just as those turtles showcase their unique traits, we too should embrace our individuality.

Our emotions, reflected in our eyes, add to our connections with others. So, let your eyes shine with authenticity and express the beauty of your true self.

Celebrate the emotions that make you human, and remember that it's okay to show vulnerability.

**After all, it's our shared feelings
that bring us closer together!**

EVERY SHELL IS DIFFERENT

I get asked often how I can tell who each of my turtles are. That's like asking a parent if they know who each twin or triplet is. Or asking a dog parent to pick out their fur baby in a park.

Every turtle's shell is different, just like we are.

Even with the six red-eared slider turtles I have, each one has a unique design. One has what looks like backwards Oklahoma shapes on her shell. One has perfectly symmetrical triangles on her shell. One is completely dark, while one has the cutest little ripples.

We are all different. Even twins have things that differentiate themselves apart from one another. It is okay to be different, and we should embrace what makes us different. That's why there are so many different species in our beautiful world!

Additionally, did you know that baby turtles have unique designs on the bottoms of their shells? Even if you don't see any differences on the tops of those teeny tiny shells, the bottoms will help you differentiate who each turtle is until they get a bit bigger.

So, no matter how young you are, how small, or how insignificant you may feel, know this: everyone is different because they are born to be different. We are here to make our mark on the world and we can't do that unless we use our uniqueness to do so.

EVER-LASTING MESSAGES

HAPPINESS BEGINS WITH A SMILE

"Do me a favor, smile." Those were the first words my future husband ever said to me.

Did you know that when you smile, your brain releases endorphins which are like natural painkillers. It helps to reduce stress, and it enhances your mood. Try it. Smile.

No matter how you are feeling right now. Hold it for a few seconds. Take a deep breath, close your eyes, and just smile.

Don't Wait for Life to Happen

Box turtles and tortoises are symbols of patience and perseverance, but they also remind us that life is meant to be lived in the present.

Don't wait for life to happen; seize the day! Just like a tortoise who ventures out into the sun, embrace every opportunity that comes your way. The journey may be slow, but each step is filled with a potential for discovery.

Remember, life is now. Every moment spent in hesitation is a moment lost. So, step out of your shell and explore your world!

Whether it's trying something new, pursuing a passion, or connecting with others, make the choice to live fully.

Just like the gentle pace of a box turtle, embrace the journey, but don't forget to enjoy the scenery along the way. The beauty of life unfolds in the here and now. So take that first step, and let the adventure begin!

EVERY STORM WILL PASS, EVENTUALLY

Are you standing at the threshold of life, staring out the window watching a storm occur? While it is smart to get out of the rain, take cover in a storm and batten down the hatches in case of high winds, eventually that storm will come to an end and you should bravely venture outside and see what is happening in the world.

In your life storms will happen, there will be dark days, lightning may strike, thunder will rumble and sometimes, tree limbs will break and fall. There may be debris to clean up, damage to repair, but you're still here. You'll survive the storm.

So step back when the dark clouds roll in. Take cover. Make plans, prepare yourself and be safe. But when the clouds part, and the sun shines through, let the light of day invite you back out into the world. Take that step.

Step out into the world, find out what you can do to move forward, and help those who can use the assistance.

No matter what, we are all here living through storms of our lives, and the more we can do to help each other, the less the next storm will frighten us. Every storm will pass.

Dive in When Life Gets Scary

When the world feels overwhelming and scary, take a cue from aquatic turtles: dive into the water. Turtles know that when life gets rough, the best response is to seek safety beneath the surface of the water.

> **The water offers them refuge,
> a place to find calm amid chaos.**

Just like turtles retreat to their aquatic haven, we too can find peace when we need it most. Instead of letting fear pull us down, we can choose to immerse ourselves in introspection, creativity, or simply a moment of stillness.

The measure of our own minds can be similarly refreshing as the cool water. Remember, it's okay to take a break and submerge yourself when things get tough.

> **Embrace that time to recharge,
> reflect, and gather your strength.**

When you're ready to resurface, you'll emerge with renewed clarity and a fresh perspective. So, when the world feels daunting, don't hesitate to dive deep. There's beauty and strength waiting for you beneath the waves.

CURIOSITY CAN BE A GOOD THING

They say curiosity killed the cat, but they've never said that about a turtle. Turtles, despite their slow pace, are naturally curious creatures.

They move cautiously, and they explore their surroundings with caution. However, they are always seeking new experiences, new insights, and new ways to navigate the world. Their curiosity is not driven by a rush to get somewhere fast, but by a desire to learn, and grow.

It's easy to feel like we should have all the answers, or that we must always be certain of our next step. But the truth is, curiosity invites us to explore the unknown, ask questions, and embrace the journey of discovery.

It encourages us to step outside our comfort zones, try new things, and view the world through fresh eyes. Curiosity with caution is good.

So, let the curiosity of the turtle inspire you.

Ask questions, explore with intention, and don't be afraid to venture into the unknown. It's through curiosity that we discover not only the world, but also our own potential.

**The more we embrace life,
the more we allow ourselves to grow.**

EXERCISE IS FUN

Exercise sounds like a bad word to me. It can feel daunting and exhausting. Like homework or even punishment. When I am told that I should exercise I tend to roll my eyes, sigh or even sulk. Why should I exercise? Don't I work hard enough already without having to sweat?

Did you know that exercise actually helps your body? Not just to lose wight, or gain muscles but it also helps you improve your mood and improve your brain function.

Did you also know that the more your exercise, the more energy you will gain and the more you will want to exercise? It's crazy, because it is exactly the opposite of what you would think. But it's true.

Turtles don't exercise the way we think of exercise. They don't jump rope, lift weights or do jumping jacks. There is no turtle yoga and I'm pretty sure they can't wear tennis shoes.

What they can do, is lift their entire house. Swim for miles at a time without stopping. Hold their breath for hours. Balance on the skinniest tree limbs, and climb to the top of any turtle pyramid.

So, if you think that a turtle's life is easy, that all they do is swim and sun bathe, you would be wrong. Everyone needs exercise, no matter what you call it or how you do it.

Your Body is a Temple, Treat it as Such

Whether you're a sea turtle, box turtle, tortoise, or aquatic turtle, that shell isn't going anywhere! It's not just their home; it's an integral part of their body. While we have skin and bones, turtles have bones and shells, their identity. Any cartoon that shows a turtle casually shedding its shell is simply misleading.

For turtles, their shell is their sanctuary, and their protection. It may get scratched, punctured, or even painted by human hands, but it remains their everything. Similarly, we must cherish and care for our own bodies, recognizing that it is all we have in this life. Turtles nurture their shells, so we should honor our bodies and avoid anything that could cause permanent harm.

Embrace self-care, and remember that your body is your most valuable asset. Treat it with the love and respect it deserves!

BE PRESENT EVERY DAY

It doesn't matter how young you are or how old you feel, every day is a gift worth celebrating. That is why they call it the present. So go out, explore, embrace the day, smile, soak it all in and be there. Just be there.

You owe it to yourself to see what God has in store for you!

COURAGE SHOWS CONFIDENCE

Speak up! This is your life. Your day. Don't be afraid to say what is on your mind. Your feelings and thoughts matter. So long as what you want to say is not intentionally hurtful, and won't cause too much strife, say what is on your mind.

Being courageous shows confidence.

SUCCESS DOESN'T HAPPEN OVERNIGHT

We're all at different stages of our lives. Some are in the beginning stages, some are towards the end. Most of us are somewhere in the middle, figuring things out and making it up as we go along. Don't judge where you are by comparing your progress with anyone else. Some may master their talents young, while others need ample life lessons to hone their skills.

Take it from the turtle, you will get there when you get there. It's as easy as that.

I Hope You Had a Turtle-ific Day!

Don't forget, you are turtle-y awesome.

Stick your neck out for others,
it's a good way to make friends.

You are shell-dom alone.

Slow down and appreciate each day.

Life is a shell-abration.

Kathleen J. Shields & Ruth the Turtle Sunbathing

Yes, that's me, sunbathing with the turtles in our turtle pond, while reading a book about turtles. The beautiful turtle on the rock is Ruth. She's been a family pet for as long as I can remember. She's super social. Since my Mom and I lived in apartments, she spent quite a bit of time in my bath tub soaking and then exploring the apartment the rest of the time. She's very used to cats and when the dogs met her for the first time, they fell in love. *What's not to love?*

I have always had turtles. My Mom and her sister raised turtles. In fact, my aunt became a veterinarian and cared for endangered desert tortoises in California. When I met my husband, I discovered he had a pet box turtle and loved turtles as well. I guess that it was meant to be.

While cultivating our turtle family we went from a 20-gallon aquarium to a 55-gallon. We then added a 75-gallon and a 90-gallon aquarium. Before long we began incorporating those plastic kiddie pools to give them more space to move around. When Intex came out with the first Easy Set pool (the blue round ones with the inflatable ring), we bought the 6-foot diameter and built a habitat for our growing aquatic family on our back porch. It had a center island and they loved it. For me, we bought a 10-foot pool for the summer.

Then one weekend while I was away at a book festival, my husband converted my 10-foot Easy Set swimming pool into the new turtle habitat upgrading them from the 6-foot. So I upgraded my 10-foot diameter pool to a 12-foot pool. Yet, even THAT swimming pool became the new turtle pond the next summer. I was fairly frustrated that I had lost my summertime fun, twice, but how could I complain – he did it for the turtles!

Next thing I knew, we were nailing together railroad ties, laying out a huge black pond liner and creating a 20-foot by 30-foot above-ground pond in the backyard, complete with island and egg-laying beach! My husband even designed an impressive filtration system with the ecological and biological needs of excessive turtle poo in mind. (Trust me, turtles poo a LOT!)

When our first baby turtle hatched, we were the proudest parents ever. We named him August after my father and the month he was born. The next year when over 30 baby turtles hatched, we were

the most generous donators to the school's science classrooms, ever. *Hey, what were we going to do with that many turtles?*

We hosted the Boy Scouts to teach them about turtles. We educated the community. We were known as the turtle family, and we were contacted by local veterinarians to adopt other people's pet turtles when the need arose. We inherited so many different turtle species that we had to increase our knowledge on each of them.

When we moved to a large ranch, we found it ironic that we'd see turtles walking across our property. It was like the turtles KNEW we were coming! Many of them were Mud turtles, a species we hadn't gotten to play with yet.

That brought forth questions like, why do we only see the Mud turtles when it's pouring down rain? Where do they go when we're in drought? And look at this teeny weenie baby Mud turtle I found!

At one point, our pastor contacted us. He had a parishioner who bought a small tortoise from a pet store and THEN did the research on the species to discover how big it was going to get. The parishioner lived in an apartment complex and couldn't raise a 200-pound tortoise, so he started asking if anyone was interested in giving a forever home to a tortoise. Of course, our pastor knew of someone – us!

Next thing I knew, we were learning about African Sulcata Tortoises, their dietary requirements, habitat needs, etc. After a couple of successful years raising Guinness, another Tortoise, Harp, came to need a home. Guess who got a brother?

It's always been turtles – so why wouldn't I want to share my fun and excitement about this species with others? Besides this book, I also wrote a book called "Turtle Diaries." It incorporates all of the love and education I've cultivated over the years. And why not write that book in the form of a diary written by a turtle? I specialize in educational children's books after all! Hence, Turtle Diaries, came to be.

I knew I wanted to share my lifetime of knowledge with the youth but I wanted it to be fun. I didn't want it to be too simple because there are a lot of types of turtles I wanted to cover. I also didn't want it to be too scientific like all of those educational turtle books that list Phylum, Classification, Etymology, Anatomy, Scientific Class, Ecology, Diet, Habitat, etc. That, to me, is a little boring. I don't want to bore a child about turtles, I want to excite them by sharing the turtles own personal stories.

But my primary goal is to educate children. I want them to know the basics. I want them to know how much work is involved. I want them to know that not all turtles make great pets. And I also want them to know that a turtle is a lifetime adoption.

Smaller turtles like Mud, Musk, Map, Diamondback Terrapins, etc. won't necessarily outgrow their tanks, but some are illegal to keep as pets. The more common red-eared Sliders will definitely out-grow their tanks, in short order, or, you take a chance of stunting their growth and causing shell defects.

They need to be fed a proper diet. Their water needs to be filtered and changed regularly. They need specific kinds of lighting and tank designed for basking and drying out. They can live to be 100 years old and if you raise them from a baby, they won't know how to care for themselves in the wild. They will be used to the food being delivered to them. They won't know how to hunt, so releasing them back into the wild, is not necessarily fair to them.

There is a lot about turtles, a lot more than you can find in this book. *There is a lot I didn't cover because some things children don't need to know, yet.** Turtle Diaries is designed to be a starting point, not the end-all educational resource. If you have a question about turtles that I didn't cover, you can probably find the answer on the internet. There is a plethora of knowledge out there, and all it takes is an inquisitive mind to want to learn the answer and your knowledge can grow!

So there you have it: Turtle Diaries and now, Have a Turtle-ific Day! I hope you enjoyed this book and hope you may consider checking out "Turtle Diaries". If you did like this, please consider leaving a review for the author and telling your friends about it. When it comes to marketing, I am only one person, but if I have a little help from each one of you, I can educate and inspire millions!

ABOUT THE AUTHOR

Kathleen J. Shields is prolific writer of multiple genres and an award-winning author having won First Place Best Educational Children's Series from the Texas Association of Authors for "The Hamilton Troll Adventures". Six book awards and counting for her long-awaited "First UniBear" rhyming children's story that she wrote when she was only ten years old, and even Christian fiction.

The Hamilton Troll series is educational. It teaches young children social skills, animal characteristics and how to handle real-life situations.

While awaiting illustrations, Shields' writes chapter books for her slightly older readers (tweens and general audiences). While still infusing education into each story, Kathleen endeavors to entertain young readers, igniting a desire to read (and maybe even write) that will span a lifetime.

Recently, Kathleen has focused on inspirational children's books and affirmation books. She endeavors to present the love of God to those who may be seeking enlightenment.

Shields' also runs a website and graphic design company called Kathleen's Graphics. She designs websites, custom logos and advertisements for businesses and authors. She can assist authors with custom book covers, interior formatting and publishing. She can put together book trailer videos, write press releases and so much more. She enjoys being challenged to learn new things.

Additionally, Kathleen writes an inspirational and educational blog regarding her endeavors as an author as well as a business woman and Christian. Her views are always light-hearted, thought-provoking or funny, and are intended to get the reader thinking.

For more information about the author, and her books, please visit: **www.KathleensBooks.com** or follow her blog: **www.KathleenJShields.com**

KATHLEEN'S BOOKS

Ghost Dogs As a toddler Jamie develops an amazing gift, the ability to see Ghost Dogs. They look just like our past pets, just a bit more transparent.

Turtle Diaries When a tortoise roams a turtle sanctuary, fun, education and challenges ensue. He keeps a daily diary of his adventures.

Dream World Defenders

Ryan and his friends enter the dream world where they can do anything they can imagine. Except... Wake up.

Zits from Outer Space A Giant Scorpion, a Crab Attack and a Killer Wolf, What do these have in common? The zits on Jared's face! Boys will be boys with active imaginations.

Ally Cat, A Tale of Survival Allison Catsworth "Ally Cat" gets knocked off of a cliff and instead of falling to her death, she transforms into a cat and lands on all four paws!

A Rainbow of Thanks Kate walks into a rainbow and is transported to various places on the planet as she tries to get back home.

The Painting Gerald is given a blank canvas, so he paints a world, one that he loves so much – it comes to life!

The First Book of a Trilogy

The Painting 2 Benjamin, Gerald's son, finds a way to be born into the Painting so he can tell the inhabitants about his father, the Painter.

The Painting 3 Nevaeh, the granddaughter, imagines herself into the painting. While she is only there in spirit, it is her desire to good that inspires others to act.

 **The Painting Trilogy Hard back** is the full collection of stories in a collector's edition hardback book with beautiful dust jacket. A must have!

 **Dandy Lion, A Legend of Love & Loss** Dandy loses a strand of hair each time he helps someone. In essence he is sowing the seeds of love by doing good deeds.

 **A Rhyme for Everything** is a poetry collection of funny, inspirational, musical and simply creative rhyming verses for any occasion.

The First UniBear A bear rescues a horse that is actually a unicorn. Then bear gets a unicorn horn on his head. This is a multiple award-winning inspirational rhyming story.

The First Unicorn
A young horse who likes to help others gets bestowed a horn making him the first unicorn. What he can do with his horn is simply miraculous.

The Etiquette of Book Selling
A how to book encouraging authors to be their best and make a good first impression.

PAWsitive Vibes, Dogs
This fun devotional connects dog emotions and real stories to motivational messages for humans to take to heart.

The Dog Who Cried Woof
Riley takes it upon himself to announce Daddy's return home, but turns it into a game that goes horribly wrong. ***Short Story eBook***

Ethan's Reception FiFi was not happy the day Ethan was brought home from the animal shelter, but Ethan was enthralled! ***Short Story eBook***

Also be sure to check out
The Hamilton Troll Adventures

Twelve fully illustrated, rhyming educational stories for bedtime up to 2nd grade. They teach social skills, animal characteristics and even science. They also increase vocabulary by providing definitions to words. There is also a Children's Cookbook, a Coloring book and a curriculum workbook to continue the education. Perfect for home school.

And for Young Adults:
The Kaitlyn Jones Trilogy

Kaitlyn Jones discovers sha has the gift of precognition, she's able to see things before they happen. She also discovers a telepathic bond with the guy who changed her life.

Mix that with a desire to help others and you have an action-packed trilogy that will keep you hooked until the end. Follow Kaitlyn through High School, her first job as a police officer.

When she became a bodyguard, joined the secret service and then became a secret agent! The adventure begins here.

How to Write, Market & Sell Children's Books
A comprehensive guide taking aspiring authors through each step of the writing, publishing and marketing process.

Her Guarded Desire
Kristen must decide between her boyfriend and her bodyguard, when the danger reemerges and they are forced on the run.

The Day Hell Froze Over
When the inhabitants of hell begin praying for some cold weather, the devil finds himself in a bind. **Short Story eBook**

Erin Go Bragh Publishing publishes various genres of books for numerous authors. Their portfolio consists of a 1200-page Vietnamese to English Dictionary, Historical fiction, an award-winning children's educational series, multiple adult novels and memoirs, tween adventure stories, as well as Christian Fiction. Their objective is to promote literacy and education through reading and writing.

www.ErinGoBraghPublishing.com
Canyon Lake, Texas